IF YOU CHANGE YOUR
WORDS,
YOU'LL CHANGE YOUR
LIFE!

"THIRTY WORD CONFESSIONS THAT
WILL TRANSFORM YOUR LIFE"

MAXINE ARLENE RYAN

IF YOU CHANGE YOUR
WORDS,
YOU'LL CHANGE YOUR
LIFE!

"THIRTY WORD CONFESSIONS THAT WILL TRANSFORM YOUR LIFE"

Copyright © 2019 Maxine Arlene Ryan

If You Change Your Words, You'll Change Your Life:
Thirty Word Confessions That Will Transform Your Life

Published by ZION Publishing House

Sioux Falls, S.D, & Washington D.C.

www.zionpublishinghouse.com

ISBN: 978-1-7336689-0-3 print
   978-1-7336689-1-0 eBook

All rights reserved. The author guarantees all contents are original and do not infringe upon the legal rights of any other person or work. No part of this book may be reproduced, distributed, or transmitted in any form or by any means – electronic, mechanical, digital, photocopy, recording, or any other—except for brief quotations in printed reviews, without the prior written permission of the publisher.

Scripture quotations taken from the Amplified® Bible (AMP), Copyright © 2015 by The Lockman Foundation
Used by permission. www.Lockman.org

Scripture quotations taken from the Amplified® Bible (AMPC), Copyright © 1954, 1958, 1962, 1964, 1965, 1987 by The Lockman Foundation. Used by permission. www.Lockman.org

Taken from the HOLY BIBLE: EASY-TO-READ VERSION © 2014 by Bible League International. Used by permission.

Scripture taken from the New King James Version®. Copyright © 1982 by Thomas Nelson. Used by permission. All rights reserved.

Printed in the United States of America

Dedication

I dedicate this book to my beautiful princess, Carisha Nicola Ryan. Carisha, I want you to know your dad and I love you so much! You are an inspiration to us, and we pray the blessings of the Lord will be on you in all that your hands have set to do. I pray that the faithful God will keep your feet from falling, and He will give you the desires of your heart!

We love you so much!
Mom and Dad!

Acknowledgements

Foremost, I would like to take this time to
acknowledge my Lord and Savior, Jesus Christ,
who is the lover of my soul, the author and
finisher of my faith. I love you, Abba Father!

I also want to say, "Thanks a million" to my
Pastors, Apostle Tony and Cynthia Brazelton,
who labor and commit themselves to teaching
and preaching the pure Word of God.
It is because of your commitment to God's
people that I've learned how valuable
my words are.
I am and will be forever grateful to you both
for your labor of love! Thank you,
and I love you both!

Table of Contents

Introduction	11
General Confession	25
Walking in True Repentance	29
Spiritual Warfare	33
Living Free from Generational Curses	39
Breaking Free from Strongholds	45
Breaking Free from the Bondage of the Mind	49
Waiting for God	55
Breaking Free from an Unforgiving Heart	59
Remaining Consistent During Testing	65
When my Enemies Rise up Against me	71
Walking through Seasons of Uncertainty	75
Children	79
Confessions for Adult Children	85
A Marriage Made in Heaven	87
Desiring to be Married	91
Overcoming Temptation	97
Overcoming the Spirit of Fear	101
Living in the Protection of God	105
Defending Healing in the Kingdom	109
Breaking Free from Ungodly Habits	115

Cultivating the Fruit of the Spirit	119
Living With Divine Purpose and Destiny	123
The Confession of a Tither	127
Walking in Debt Freedom	131
Walking in Kingdom Prosperity	135
Believing God for Employment	141
Living with Good Health	145
Standing in Faith for an Unsaved Loved One	149
Defeating Unbelief, Doubt, and Frustration	153
Breaking Through to a Successful Business	157
Bonus Confessions	161
Standing in the Gap for our Leaders (Government)	163
Breaking Free From the Spirit of Homosexuality	167
Overcoming the Spirit of Depression	171
Defeating Loneliness	175
Emergency Numbers	179

Introduction

Praying and confessing words of faith is essential for living a victorious Christian life. Jesus is the High Priest over our faith confessions. He is seated on the right hand of the Father, gives every believer all authority through His Word, His blood, and through His name. Every time a believer makes a confession based on the Word of God, he or she has the whole authority of Christ behind him or her (Hebrews 3:1). Activating the Word of God with prayers of confession is necessary in the life of every born-again believer. Our High Priest, Jesus, backs up every word that we speak.

Once the Word of God is released, *it brings forth spirit, and it brings forth life* (John 6:63). We have ministering angels standing guard, watching over every word we speak. As soon as the Word of God is released, our ministering angels go and work on our behalf (Psalm 103:20). So, when a believer makes the right confession, we invite ministering angels to manifest the glory of God through the Word of God.

The Bible says, "For the word of God is living and active and full of power [making it operative, energizing, and effective]. It is sharper than any two-edged sword, penetrating as far as the division of the soul and spirit [the completeness of a person], and of joints and marrow [the deepest parts of our nature], exposing and judging the very thoughts and intentions of the heart" (Hebrews 4:12 AMP). As soon as believers confess the Word of God, a two-edged sword goes out of our mouths. When confessing the Word, we must not waver in our confession because, if we waver, we will not receive anything from God. A person that wavers in his confession *is unstable in all his ways* (James 1:6-7).

Before God can deliver anything into the hands of the believer, first, it must be declared with our mouths. The believer shapes their future by making confessions based on the Word of God. The Bible says *the tongue is like the pen of a ready writer* (Psalm 45:1). God has already written our life; He sees us from the beginning to the end; however, when we make confessions based on God's promises for our lives, we come into agreement with Him, by declaring what He has already written about us.

INTRODUCTION

God Made Man in His Image—To Carry His Power

God wanted the ability to extend His kingdom here on earth, so He created man and gave him *dominion* (Hebrew word is *radah*, which means to rule, authority, dominate and tread down) here on earth (Genesis 1:26). Elohim, in Genesis 1, spoke forth the firmament, earth, plants, sun, moon, stars, and sea with the living creatures in it, and the animals. When God formed the earth, God said, "Let there be," and there was. So, the heavens and earth were created from God's voice, from His very Words. God spoke the entire universe into being. So, if God is the *all-powerful* speaking spirit, then so are we. *As Jesus is, so are we in this world* (1 John 4:17). We are powerful speaking spirits!

God's dominion was binding when He spoke. Every Word He spoke manifested into something. In Genesis 1:26, when *God said, "let us (The Trinity) make man in our own image,"* the spirit of man was created. Then, as we see later in Genesis, Chapter 2, God formed man out of the dust of the ground, and He breathed into him the breath of life, and man became a living soul. God made the man with His Words, hands, and dust from the earth. He made men like himself. Literally, God duplicated himself into the form of a man. A man (spirit) was created in the image and likeness of God.

I could only imagine when God created the first (godman) Adam; all creation stood at attention to watch this astonishing event. If my imagination could run wild, earth stood still as it welcomed Adam (the first godman), who would rule the earth and would have authority and dominion in the earth. Adam would use his words to give every animal a name, and when he spoke, it was so. Adam had the ability to create what he desired with his very own words. In the same way, believers have the ability that Adam had when God created him.

Everything that Adam spoke with his mouth became a reality. Today, because human beings are spirit, soul, and body, the words that we speak are extremely important. Just like God, what we speak will come to pass. As human beings, our words carry the ability to create *life or death* (Proverbs 18:21). We are speaking spirits because God created us to be like Him. As I said earlier, God has given us the ability to reign and rule in this earth, and one of the ways we must rule is by *word-based* confessions.

INTRODUCTION

God is Waiting for us to Exercise our Authority in the Earth

Most Christians believe they are waiting on God to solve their problems in their lives, communities, homes, cities, or nation. In fact, they say that God is in control, but this is not all truth. He is in control through His sons, *and creation waits in eager expectation for the sons of God to be revealed* (Roman 8:19). I believe, without a shadow of a doubt, God is waiting for believers to step into position. He did not give us the ability to rule, and then take it back. No way! If God is in control of the earth, how do you explain when a three-year-old is left in the care of her mother's boyfriend, and the boyfriend rapes and kills this precious gift? Most people might be saying, "Where was God then?" Remember, Satan is the god of this world, the accuser of the brethren, who has invaded this planet. But Jesus took back this authority that was taken by Satan and restored mankind back to his original state when He first created Adam.

This is why we cannot be ignorant of who we are. We must stand and *fight the good fight of faith, so that we can lay hold of eternal life* (I Timothy 6:12). The earth waits for believers to take their place and to rule the earth. The kingdom of God is within us. Every born-again, spirit-filled believer carries the presence of God. Our bodies are the temples of God.

God is a promise-keeper. He will not go back on His Word. God gave man dominion on the earth, and because His Word is binding, He will not intervene without an invitation. A godman here on earth must invite God into their earthly affairs by Word-based confessions, prayer, worship, and praise. We must declare and decree the Word that will release angelic hosts. God sent His angelic hosts to bless us, and He himself will show up in our earthly situation. We must give God permission; He will not come in uninvited.

The Power and Purpose of Our Confessions

When a believer speaks, either an angel is working on their behalf, or a demon, depending on whatever word is spoken. This is why confessing the Word is critical in the life of the believer. *Confessions are when we say the same things that God says or agree with what God says about us and not what our circumstances look like or appear to be.* Every situation we are facing, the answer to that situation can be found in the Word of God.

INTRODUCTION

I have come in contact with some believers who want a quick fix. They don't want to take the time to read, study, meditate, or confess the Word. They want leaders to read, study, meditate, and confess the Word for them. Here is a piece of gold I found in the Word. I call it *gold* because it is the answer to every prayer a believer can pray. It is a key to the kingdom that unlocks every door. "My son, pay attention to what I say. Listen closely to my words. Don't let them out of your sight. Never stop thinking about them. These words are the secret of life and health to all who discover them. Above all, be careful what you think because your thoughts control your life." (Proverbs 4:20-23 ERV).

Wow! I feel like shouting! These few verses just gave us the key to a successful life and good health. The Word of God says the Word must be kept before our eyes, ears, in our thoughts, and in our hearts because it is the key to good life.

One of the reasons I wrote this book is because I am a lover of the Word of God, and I recognized, years ago, that nothing happens in my life without saying and decreeing it first. The tongue has the ability to bless or curse. We must choose to speak the blessings of the Lord over our lives in every situation. If we desire to live in the fullness of the blessing of the Lord, we must activate what has already been given to us spiritually into our natural world by speaking the Word.

When we speak death, the portal of hell is opened in our lives. In other words, whatever we speak becomes a reality before our very own eyes. The words we speak come from the depths of the heart of the believer. For Scripture says, "For what has been stored up in your hearts will be heard in the overflow of your words!" (Matthew 12:34 TPT). If you would like to know what's in a person's heart, just sit down and have a conversation with them. Whatever is coming out of their mouths is coming directly from what is in their hearts in abundance. When you change your words, your words change your life—either for good or for bad.

Watch What You Confess

"For by thy words thou shalt be justified, and by thy words thou shalt be condemned" (Matthew 12:37 KJV). As believers, we will either be justified or acquitted, or we will be condemned or sentenced because of what we choose to speak. We must think before we speak and take what comes out of our mouths seriously.

INTRODUCTION

I have met many believers who do not take this kingdom principle seriously. They say things like, "*I am getting old!*" "*My foot is killing me!*" "*I am broke!*" "*I cannot afford that!*" "*I am going to be this way until I die because I am too old to change!*" The Bible says *the tongue is the pen of a ready writer,* so when we speak, we are writing the destiny of our lives (Psalm 45:1).

Moses led the Israelites out of Egypt; the children of Israel are the descendants of Abraham who died out in the wilderness. The Israelites declared with their own mouths their destiny, and exactly what they said came to pass. Consequently, many of them died in their wilderness experience. What does this have to do with you? I'm glad you asked. Can you imagine dying in your wilderness experience because of what's coming out of your mouth? There is no way we can speak whatever we please, and break the strongholds of the past, and still receive what God has for us.

The Bible says, "Gentle words are a tree of life; and a deceitful tongue crushes the spirit" (Proverbs 15:4 NLT). When we confess the Word of God, God takes our words and creates fruit with them. Then, we experience victory over defeat, and good fruit is produced. God watches over His Word and performs what is spoken out of our mouths. We must therefore, activate the blessings of God over our lives by confessing what has already been given to us by faith.

Our Words are Seeds

The Bible says *God's Word is an incorruptible seed* (I Peter 1:23). Every time seeds are released, they go directly into our hearts and then, into the atmosphere. The Word of God says in Genesis 8:22 (AMP), "While the earth remains, seedtime and harvest, cold and heat, summer and winter, day and night shall not cease."

In order to have a harvest, the sower must sow the Word by confessing the Word of God until it grows into a tree or until manifestation shows up. Warning! When you begin to declare Word-based confessions consistently, don't be alarmed if you experience a bit of turbulence. This does not mean your confessions are not working. Press forward! When the Word is *sown into good ground, your heart*, (James 1:21), *Satan comes immediately and tries to steal the Word* (Mark 4:15). He does this by trying to have us walk in the spirit of offense, and even tries to tempt us to sin. Have you ever noticed when you hear a good Word, and you receive it by faith, it seems like all hell breaks loose in your life? Well, most times, it is a struggle to even remember the Word you have heard. This happens because the devil is after that Word because he knows, very well, if the Word that is planted takes root, it has the ability to create a harvest. So, he tries everything in his power to frustrate us, so that our seed won't grow into a tree. This is why it is important for us to protect the Word that is sown in our hearts, so we can produce a harvest beyond our wildest dreams. If you are a born-again believer, you have the ability to produce life with the words you speak.

While declaring and decreeing *faith* words, it is important that we only say what God says and nothing else! We must speak His Word back to Him because His Word will never return to Him void. "So will my word be which goes out of My mouth; It will not return to Me void (useless, without result), without accomplishing what I desire, and without succeeding in the matter for which I sent it" (Isaiah 55:11 AMP). The Word of God will always produce a harvest when sown in good ground. We cannot be moved by what we see or hear, or what it appears to be; we are only to be moved by the Word of God. We must choose to believe the Word of God at all costs. It must be first place and the final authority in our lives. We cannot speak one thing, then live contrary to what we are confessing. Our lives must be pleasing to God.

According to Romans 10:9, *if we confess with our mouth that Jesus is Lord, and believe in our hearts that God raised him from the dead, we will be saved.* It is by saving faith that we received Jesus as our personal Savior. We believe with our hearts, and we confess with our mouths. In the very same way that confession is made unto salvation, we must confess the Word in order to obtain our deliverance. In Romans 10:11, the Word of God declares *that none of us who believe or confess in Jesus will be put to shame.* I feel like shouting! If we remain constant and don't give up on our confession, we will *not* be disappointed. We will reap, if we faint not.

We must remember words are spirits, and it is critical that we release the right spirit in the atmosphere. Furthermore, when our minds do not go through the process of renewing, our toxic thoughts become a reality in our lives. We can change this when we meditate (Hebrew word *hagah*, which means: muse, ponder, imagine, mutter, speak) *on the Word of God day and night* (Joshua 1:8). The Word must be kept in our eyes daily. Then, His thoughts, which are His Words, become our thoughts.

I challenge you for the next thirty days to take a journey through this book. Before you start your day, pray and make Word-based confessions in order to make a spiritual transfer of what has already been given to you in the natural. The secret of having a great future is found in your daily routine. This book focuses on every aspect of your life. Stay consistent, so these confessions become a part of who you are. Let this be a start of a brand-new life in God. Also, what you do every day determines the quality of your future. Remember, faith has to be in your heart and mouth (Romans 10:8). Before manifestation takes place, you must declare it with your mouth before you can see it with your eyes. So, in the name of Jesus, I call heaven and earth to witness this day against you that *I have set before you, life and death, the blessings and curses; therefore, choose life, that you and your descendants may live* (Deuteronomy 30:19). Hallelujah!

Note for the Reader: Most confessions in this book begin with an explanation. Where there is an (open parentheses), fill that space in with a name or speak in tongues. If you have not been baptized in the Holy Spirit, or if you don't believe in speaking in tongues, there is no problem. Feel free to pray and clap your hands instead. The Bible says *he teaches our hands to war, so that a bow of steel is broken by our arms* (Psalm 18:34). As you pray, your hands are doing battle, and chains are being broken in the name of Jesus.

General Confession

Father, right now in the name of Jesus, *I gird my loins with the belt of truth. I put on the breastplate of righteousness. I cover my feet with the preparation of the gospel of peace. I take up the shield of faith. I place on my head the helmet of salvation, and I take up the sword of the spirit, which is the Word of God* (Ephesians 6:10-18*). I present my body a living sacrifice, holy and acceptable* unto you, Father, *which is my reasonable service* (Romans 12:1).

I stand in my authority on this day, and I command every second heaven activity that is trying to hinder my confession from reaching the third heaven, to be unblocked in the name of Jesus *(Speak in the Holy Spirit or clap your hands)*. I dispatch my angels of God to go right now and fight on my behalf *(Speak in the Holy Spirit or clap your hands)* (Daniel 10). I stand against *all principalities and powers, against the rulers of the darkness of this world*, and *against spiritual wickedness in high places* (Ephesians

6:12). I command you to bow your knees now in Jesus' name. Every demonic or satanic activity in my life, I release (fire, fire).

I render Satan's work powerless, and I decree and declare you have no power over me. I declare that every work and plan, and all negative words, thoughts, actions, traps, and assignments that have been sent out for me, are returning to the sender now.

I release *fire* on every witch, warlock, negative words, satanic altars, strongholds, third eye, and hindering spirits that have been sent out to block my manifestation from coming forward, to *blow up* now, in Jesus' name. I command every satanic womb that was created to stop or block my progress, to miscarry right now. I release myself from every ungodly tie and soul ties that have connected themselves to me *(Speak in the Holy Spirit or clap your hands)*.

I am growing every day in *wisdom and stature and favor with God and with man* according to Luke 2:52. I am walking in the wisdom of God now *(Speak in the Holy Spirit or clap your hands)*. I decree and declare my coast is enlarging now. My *gift is making room for me and bringing me before great men* (Proverbs 18:16). I am a carrier of the glory of God, and anywhere I set my feet the glory of God will be there. Every atmosphere that does not line up with the Word of God will shift because I showed up. I believe because I am *in Christ that I am the seed of Abraham and the heir according to the promise that God made with Abraham* in Galatians 3:29. I walk in my spiritual inheritance; I am highly favored, God's favorite child, prosperous, healthy, wealthy, and rich. I am blessed spiritually, mentally, physically, and financially, and it is the will of God that I multiply in every area. I am anointed, *chosen and royal, and I belong to a holy nation* according to I Peter 2:9. I am God's very own possession. I walk in the supernatural power and protection that God has already given to me. I decree I will not die before my time, and I will die empty. Every accident, fire, misfortune, and natural disaster that the enemy has planned to come my way, I destroy it now by fire. I decree that everything my hands touch today has already been blessed! I thank you, Jesus. I believe I receive now. Amen!

Walking in True Repentance

The Greek word for repentance is *metanoeo*; it means: *to change one's mind, to repent; to change one's mind for the better.* True repentance starts with first admitting we have done wrong. Once we realize we have done wrong, we must confess or repent for our wrongdoing. Then, after we have acknowledged with our mouth, we must decide to change our direction. I heard a great woman of God say, "Repentance is a gift and not a punishment." She is correct because God gave us this gift of true repentance, so we can live free. Most often, we say we are sorry for our wrong, but we do not change our direction. Like a dog goes back to his vomit, we go back to our sin. If the individual does not change his or her mind and direction, then we cannot say true repentance took place. God will heal those broken places in our lives through the gift of repentance.

Joseph is an example to us. When sin presented itself to him, he ran away without looking back. This must be our position as sin tries to capture us. If we fall in sin, we should get up, dust ourselves off, repent, and make a decision to turn away and don't go back to that sin. True repentance includes making a decision not to do that thing again. We see another perfect illustration in the Word of God in the book of Jonah.

The Bible says after Jonah walked through the city and declared that the city would be destroyed, the King of Nineveh called a fast, and all the people repented. They did not only say they were sorry, but they changed direction. True repentance is committing our hearts totally to God and deciding in our hearts never to do it again. In I John 1:9-10 (KJV), the Word of God says, "If we confess our sins, he is faithful and just to forgive us our sins, and to cleanse us from all unrighteousness. If we say that we have not sinned, we make him a liar, and his word is not in us." Now, it is time to repent!

Confession for True Repentance

Most graceful and everlasting Father, according to Psalm 51:1, *Have mercy on me, O God, according to thy loving-kindness and thy tender mercies.* I ask you to forgive me for all my known and unknown sins. Wash me and cleanse me from all unrighteousness. I have acknowledged my transgressions. O, most loving Father, your Word says if *I confess my sins, you are faithful and just to forgive me* (I John 1:9). So, right now, Master, I admit I have sinned against you. I have (fill in the blank). I ask you, Father, to wash me with your blood and make *me whiter than snow. Create in me a clean heart and renew a right spirit within me* (Psalm 51:7). Oh, Father, your Word declares that if I repent and turn to you, my sins will be wiped out. I repent of my wrongful acts (known and unknown) against you or anyone else. I realize if I hide my faults, I will not prosper. So, I make a decision right now to turn from my wicked ways so I can receive mercy. According to Psalm 139:23-24 (KJV), "Search me, O God, and know my heart: try me, and know my thoughts: And see if there be any wicked way in me and lead me in the way everlasting." *Give me a willing mind and heart to obey your Word* (Psalm 51:2). O, gracious Jesus, rebuild a firm, stable, and unwavering spirit within me. I choose to turn away from (fill in the blank) now. Father, your Word says, *if I draw nigh to you, you will draw nigh to me* (James 4:8). Take me deeper in you; I long to please you and serve you all the days of my life. I surrender to you, and I give you all of me. I give you my spirit, soul and body to your keeping. I receive, by faith, the freedom Jesus made available for me over two thousand years ago. Thank you, *(Speak in the Holy Spirit or clap your hands)* LORD, for forgiving my past, present, and future sins, in Jesus' name! I believe I am free!

Spiritual Warfare

Every believer must engage in spiritual warfare to live a victorious life on earth. When God created man, He placed man in the Garden of Eden and gave him authority and dominion in the earth. Lucifer was a cherub; he was ordained and anointed by God as the mighty, angelic guardian. He had access to the holy mountain of God, and he walked among the stones of fire (Ezekiel 28:14). He had a very important position in heaven. However, instead of using his talent to serve God, he wanted to be like the Most High God—The One who created him. So, he led a rebellion with one-third of the angelic hosts. Many say there was a great battle in heaven, but I am not convinced. Lucifer and a third of the angels stood no chance against Michael, the archangel of the Lord. They were kicked out of heaven, and they invaded this planet, called earth. That is why we are in this great battle called "Spiritual Warfare" today.

Satan stole the authority from Adam. But God sent His only son, Jesus, to restore it back to humankind. Jesus took the authority back from Satan. He not only took back the authority. He defeated hell, death, and the grave. Before He ascended at the right hand of the Father, Jesus gave every born-again believer the authority in His Word, His name, and through His blood. This left Satan—the prince of the air, the great dragon, serpent, devil, the evil one—*powerless*. Jesus defeated, dethroned, disarmed, and destroyed Satan's authority. The only rule Satan now has is through principalities, powers, rulers of darkness, and spiritual wickedness. He does not have authority over us, unless we give it to him.

Satan is a spirit and he needs a body. He can only operate through a person who allows him to use them. This is why we must stop being timid and refuse to have him use our temple and join the fight against him. Our bodies are the *temple of the Holy Spirit* according to I Corinthians 6:19. Our spirit is holy, and it is where the Spirit of God dwells. Our souls are the inner court, and our bodies are the outer court. This is why we must refuse to allow Satan to use our temple to sin against God. We must realize, according to Ephesians 6:12, that the fight is not against *flesh and blood* (people), but *against principalities, against powers, against rulers of the darkness of this world, against spiritual wickedness in high places.* When we are fighting spiritual warfare, we must remember people are just instruments; the fight is against satanic or demonic forces. The word *warfare* means, according to the *Vine's Complete Expository Dictionary,* a spiritual conflict. We must remember that the battle is already won, and we are not fighting for victory. We are defending what Jesus has already given us. We are fighting from victory.

The believer must fight to the finish, and we must stay strong because God has given us weapons in order to keep Satan under our feet. Remember, He has given us His Word, His blood, and His name, Jesus, as our spiritual weapons. Also, we have His armor to keep us protected from the enemy. But we must choose to put on the whole armor of God while we are engaging ourselves in battle (Ephesians 6:11-17). The battleground is in our minds. So, when Satan throws thoughts our way to trap us, we must decide to cast down every imagination he throws our way and bring it to the obedience of the Word of God (II Corinthians 10:5). Believers must be prepared at all times and take up our weapons of truth, righteousness, peace, faith, and salvation with prayers, and we must continually remain in the fight. This fight against spiritual wickedness will persist; *it is a life-or-death fight to the finish against the devil and all his angels* (Ephesians 6:12 MSG).

Confession for Spiritual Warfare

(Speak in the Holy Spirit and clap your hands) I stand in the authority Jesus has given me, and I put on the whole armor of God. I put on truth, righteousness, peace, faith, and salvation, and I cover myself now with the blood of Jesus, according to Ephesians 6:10-17. I cancel every assignment that has been sent against me. I counter-attack it with the blood of Jesus, and I frustrate every evil plan of the enemy against me. I declare *no weapon that has been formed against me will prosper, and every tongue that has been raised up against me is condemned* (Isaiah 54:17).

I destroy every evil assignment that has been set up against me, which includes voodoo dolls, third eye, and every demonic or satanic altar with my name on it. I command it to *blow up*, now in Jesus' name! Every devil that flies, crawls, swims, creeps by day and by night, I call down *the consuming fire of* Esh Oklah (Hebrews 12:29) (fire, fire, fire, fire) to burn you up. Every evil decree that has been sent out with black magic, and every work of the enemy against me, I command it to be destroyed by (fire, fire, fire) *(Speak in the Holy Spirit and clap your hands.)*

I declare *greater is He that is inside me than he that is in this world* (I John 4:4). I speak to the spirits of waster, emptier, not enough, lack, poverty, stagnation, and every diabolical spirit that is in operation in my life to die now. I command you to commit suicide in the name of Jesus. I denounce you, and I declare you have no power over me *(Speak in the Holy Spirit and clap your hands)!*

I speak right now over the atmosphere, and I command the heavens to *be opened* right now in the name of Jesus. I command open doors, riches, purpose, prosperity, fulfilled dreams, the wisdom of God, increase, promotion, favor, and an abundance of blessings to fall on me now. I decree this is my season of release, goodness, visitation, and demonstration of the power of God in my life *(Speak in the Holy Spirit and clap your hands)*.

I command every spiritual attack that is planned against me to die by fire (fire, fire, fire)! I take captivity over every plan and scheme of the enemy in my life and the life of my family, and I command it to die from its root, and I release the fire of God to burn up every destructive plan in the mind of the enemy. I declare divine recovery in every area of my life!

IF YOU CHANGE YOUR WORDS, YOU'LL CHANGE YOUR LIFE!

(Pray in the Holy Spirit and clap your hands)! I decree that my enemies are being confounded and put to shame now. *(Speak in the Holy Spirit and clap your hands)* Say, "Thank you, Father, for *watching over your word to perform it* (Jeremiah 1:12)." I receive and believe I am free in Jesus' name. Amen!

Living Free from Generational Curses

Is there such a thing for a born-again, spirit-filled believer to be bound by generational curses? Over the years, I have met believers who say that, because Jesus Christ has broken the curse, we do not experience generational curses. It is true that Jesus has broken the curse and that believers are no longer cursed. However, I have encountered countless believers who have experienced the same sicknesses their natural mothers and fathers have dealt with. Here is an example of what I mean. Years ago, when I first gave my life to Christ, I met a man of God who lost his father and two uncles, around the same age, to heart disease. Then, if that wasn't bad enough, when this man of God reached a certain age, doctors told him, he too, appeared to be developing heart disease. But heart disease didn't know this man of God had a praying wife, who knew her identity in Christ. She prayed and fought in the Word and broke the cycle that was trying to take out her husband before his time. Today, he is still alive.

Naturally, this man's body seemed to move in the direction of heart disease because his human body automatically takes on the DNA of his earthly father. We know this to be true because the man in this instance—when he became a certain age—started to feel changes in his body that were tied to his earthly DNA. I have come across several believers who have made it up in their minds that, because of their natural parents' DNA, they must live with a particular curse or illness for the rest of their lives.

These believers fail to realize that Jesus has already redeemed them from the curse of their forefathers. Jesus Christ, the anointed One, has already broken the curse in their lives. We have a blood-bought right, as believers, to reject the DNA of our natural forefathers and make an exchange with Christ's DNA. The Bible says that Christ has redeemed us from the curse of the law, being made a curse for us. *For it is written, cursed is every man that hangs on a tree* (Galatians 3:13). Christ has purchased the freedom of every born-again believer, so generational curses do not belong to us because *we are a new creation in Christ Jesus* (II Corinthians

5:17). We are no longer guilty because of the sins of our forefathers. The price was paid in full, and every believer is free from the curse of the law.

This woman of God who prayed over her husband knew her inheritance, and she wasn't going to sit back and allow her husband to be taken by heart disease. Moreover, God has given us the ability *to choose either life or death, blessings or curses* (Deuteronomy 30:19). So, we must take a stand by faith, and choose life and the blessings of the LORD in our lives.

Once we identify if there is anything in our DNA that has the potential to be transferred to us, we must exchange our DNA with the DNA of Christ. This is done by taking ownership of what Jesus has done for us by speaking the Word of God, praying, and meditating on the Word, so that our thoughts become God's thoughts. This is essential because the Word of God says, "For as he thinketh in his heart, so is he," (Proverbs 23:7 KJV). Instead of saying, *"I am going to die at fifty because both of my parents died at fifty with cancer,"* we say, *"I will live and not die, and I will declare what the Lord has done* (Psalm 118:17). *With long life He will satisfy me and show me His salvation* (Psalm 91:16). This is an essential part of deliverance because our mouths and thoughts must come into agreement with what we are believing God for.

We are free spiritually, but we must defend our freedom by employing our spiritual weapons. Remember, we are not fighting for victory, and we are not struggling to break generational curses because Jesus has already won us the victory. We must come into agreement with the Word and defend what has already been made available for us through faith, prayer, and confession; this way, we take ownership of what is already ours.

Confession for Living in Freedom from Generational Curses

Father, *(Speak in the Holy Spirit or clap your hands)*, I believe by faith that Jesus has already paid the price for me because He hung on the cross (Galatians 3:13). I believe I am free from every generational curse from my mother's house and my father's house. I declare and decree *I am the righteousness of God* (II Corinthians 5:21), the son or daughter of Abraham because I am in Christ (Galatians 3:29), *and greater is He that is within me than he that is in this world* (I John 4:4). I denounce the DNA of my natural ancestors, and I take the DNA of Christ. Every curse, soul tie, ungodly altar, and evil covenant that was passed down to me or the lives of my children *(Speak in the Holy Spirit or clap your hands)* from our forefathers, I denounce you, and I declare you have no power over me nor the lives of my children.

Jesus is LORD over my health, finances, bloodline, children, mind, body, and over my emotions. I command every ungodly covenant to miscarry from the womb. I denounce every cycle of rejection and abuse—sexual, physical, mental, and verbal; and all heartbreak, incest, and molestation that has been assigned to my bloodline; I curse you now by *fire*. I renounce every ungodly practice and all iniquities in my bloodline. I decide now to settle all ties with my past, and I forgive those who have hurt and taken advantage of me. I forgive (fill in the name here) right now, and I let it go. I declare I am free from my past hurts and failures, and I am looking forward to having a great future in God.

I curse poverty, lack, the spirit of infirmity, the spirit of depression, and every satanic and demonic spirit in my bloodline, and I loose your effects on me and the lives of my children. I stand in the power that Jesus has given me, and I declare Jesus was cursed in my place. So, today, because He was cursed, I am free *(Speak in the Holy Spirit or clap your hands)*. I believe I am redeemed from the curse of the law, and I declare right now that every generational curse in my bloodline has been broken and has no power over me. Thank you, Jesus, because of your unselfish and unconditional love, I am free from the sins of my forefathers *(Speak in the Holy Spirit or clap your hands).* I thank you, Father, I will never be broke another day in my life in the name of Jesus. Amen!

Breaking Free from Strongholds

A stronghold according to *The Merriam-Webster's Dictionary and Thesaurus* is a fortified place. It is a wall, a mindset or a pattern that keeps us stagnated, and it is contrary to the Word of God. *Stronghold* is a New Testament Greek word, which means "fortress." Some translate it as a prison. Satan's purpose is to use strongholds to keep us in a spiritual prison so we will not receive anything from God.

Our thoughts bear fruit to whatsoever it is we're thinking because they are tied to our soul—our mind, our will, and our emotions. So, if the enemy can keep us in the prison of a stronghold, we can't receive anything from God because a man's thoughts determine who he is or who he becomes. If you are dealing with a stronghold in your life, you must know this is a foothold for the devil to stop you from receiving your breakthrough or deliverance. We must make a decision to commit ourselves to break loose from this fortress. The Word of God says, "For the weapons of our warfare are not carnal, (fleshly—*emphasis added*) but mighty through God to the pulling down of strongholds" (II Corinthians 10:4 KJV). Believers cannot destroy strongholds if we are fighting with earthly weapons; we must fight with spiritual weapons in order to pull down strongholds. Strongholds fall when believers fight the good fight of faith and use our spiritual weapons (The Word of God) to defeat the enemy of his or her minds. We must confess the Word because *it is spirit and life* (John 6:63), and *it is sharper than any two-edged sword* (Hebrews 4:12). Believers must get violent in their prayers. Matthew 11:12 tells us *the kingdom of heaven suffers violence, and the violent take it by force*. We must take our breakthrough by force because Satan won't just give it to us. We must *take it*, forcefully! Adding praise and fasting to our Word-based confessions is essential because praise will confuse the enemy. Once we use these weapons and stay consistent, the prison walls will fall, layers at a time.

Confession for Breaking Free from Strongholds

I speak to the stronghold of (fill in stronghold here) in my life, and I declare you have no power over me. I overcame *by the blood of the lamb and the words of my testimony* (Revelation 12:11). *(Speak in the Holy Spirit and clap your hands)*. I speak to every stronghold in my life, and I command you to bow your knees now to the name of Jesus. *(Pray in the Holy Spirit and clap your hands)*. For, though I am in the flesh, I do not war after the flesh, so I decree that the *weapons of my warfare are not carnal, but mighty through God to the pulling down of every stronghold* in my life (II Corinthians 10:4). So, I pull down every stronghold *now*.

I plead the blood of Jesus over my mind, and I break the strongholds of (fill in stronghold here) *(Speak in the Holy Spirit and clap your hands)*. I command every demonic and satanic forces that has held my mind hostage and kept me in prison to receive the *consuming fire* of God now in the name of Jesus (Hebrews 12:29). *(Speak in the Holy Spirit and clap your hands). No weapon formed against me will prosper, and every tongue that has risen up against me I command* (Isaiah 54:17) it to *fall*, and I stand in my authority and breakthrough the prison bars the enemy has set up for me. *Many are the afflictions of the righteous* man, but thank you, Father, you have already delivered me from the (fill in stronghold here) (Psalm 34:19).

I break free from every hindering spirit that is trying to stop my purpose, progress, growth, and development in God. I decree right now the voice of limitation has been silenced, and you have no power over me *(Speak in the Holy Spirit or clap your hands)*. I bind the strong man, and I loose my mind, soul, desires, and emotions. I denounce every emotional, cultural, national, religious, and denominational stronghold that has been assigned to my life. I render the enemy's work *powerless*, and I declare I am free. I call heaven and earth to witness this day against you, Satan. I am choosing life *(Speak in the Holy Spirit or clap your hands)*, and I declare that my life will never be the same. I declare that the strongholds of (fill in stronghold here) have been broken and have no power over me, in Jesus' name. Amen!

Breaking Free from the Bondage of the Mind

Mankind is a threefold being- *spirit, soul, and body* (I Thessalonians 5:23). When a believer receives Jesus as his personal Savior, *old things are passed away, and behold all things become new* (II Corinthians 5:17). The spirit of the living God comes into him and makes His home on the inside of the new believer. This is very significant.

Have you ever come in contact with a believer who has been born again for many years, but they appeared as if they are not saved because of their character and what comes out of their mouth? The logical explanation for this is the man's spirit is complete, but his soul, which is the inner court, has to go through the process of renewal in order for it to be saved. The soul needs to be renewed from the fallen man, Adam-way of thinking. The mind according to the *Vine's Complete Expository Dictionary*, the seat of reflective consciousness, comprising the faculties of perception and understanding, and those of feeling and determining. If the man only thinks negatively, then he will speak negatively and have negative results because his thoughts become fruitful. Even so, our thoughts determine our actions.

The devil's job is to keep us bound to the world's way of thinking, so our actions will be (worldly) fleshly. I believe our thoughts are seeds and, whether good or bad, they will grow into a harvest—that is good or bad. The Apostle Paul urges us not to conform (Greek meaning is to *fashion alike*) to this world, but be ye transformed (Greek meaning is *change* or *transfigure*) *by the renewing of your mind, that ye may prove what is that good, acceptable, and perfect will of God* (Romans 12:2 AMP). Each day, an individual's thoughts are loaded with tons of information that are either coming from the voice of deity, humanity, or the voice of Satan. If you thought before today that a thought is just a thought, I have come to tell you, you are mistaken.

Thoughts determine the outcome of your life. If you only think negatively, you will have a negative life. To have a victorious life as a believer, every believer must filter out negative thoughts that are from Satan and get involved in the spiritual battle that is going on in their mind. Every thought from Satan must *be held captive to the Word of God and brought into the obedience of the Word of God* (II Corinthians 10:5). So, when a seed is deposited in our minds by Satan, we have a choice to make. Either that seed will grow into a plant and soon manifest into our actions, or it will die because we will kill it by opening our mouths and decreeing the Word of God over it.

When thoughts are deposited in a believer mind, he or she must ask themselves this question: Is it true, *honest, just, pure, lovely, of a good report, virtuous, and praiseworthy?* (Philippians 4:8). If our thoughts are aligned with what is listed above, then we will create a pure result, and we will be on our way to living a life that is pleasing to God. Every born-again believer has the new nature of God, so because we have His nature, we have His mind, according to I Corinthians 2:16. In fact, people don't lose their mind overnight. When a person loses their mind, this means that a harvest has manifested from evil thoughts, and Satan has taken full control of the person's mind. The mind becomes possessed by demonic spirits when an individual neglects to get involved in the battle and, as a result, their mind becomes Satan's territory.

Completely renewing our minds will probably take a lifetime. But, we must make a decision to begin the process by using the Word to fight the good fight of faith.

Confessions for the Mind

Heavenly Father, your Word says, "For those who live according to the flesh set their minds on the things of the flesh, but those who live according to spirit, the things of the spirit." So, according to Romans 8:4 (NKJV), I fix my mind not on what is seen, but on the unseen. *(Pray in the Holy Spirit or clap your hands).* I wage war against every evil thought that is not of you *(Pray in the Holy Spirit or clap your hands).* I am no longer conforming to this world, but I am transformed because my mind is going through the process of renewal. I am not moved by what I see, but I am only moved by the Word of God. I hold every thought captive from Satan, and *I cast down every ungodly imagination that is trying to exalt itself against the knowledge of God* (II Corinthians 10:5) *(Pray in the Holy Spirit or clap your hands).* I bind every plan, plot, and every satanic and demonic spirit that is trying to sabotage my mind. I declare that I have the *mind of Christ*, and I loose my mind from every bondage of Satan *(Speak in the Holy Spirit or clap your hands)*. I believe my mind is at peace because your Word declares you *will keep me in perfect peace, whose mind is stayed on you because I trust in you* (Isaiah 26:3), and I receive God's peace now, in Jesus' name!

(Pray in the Holy Spirit and clap your hands). I decree and declare I am no longer controlled by the flesh because when I am controlled by the flesh, my mind pursues those things that gratify the flesh. So, I decree I am walking and living after the Spirit. I set my mind on those things which are above, and I denounce every ungodly thought that has made its way into my heart. I renounce this world's way of thinking, and I believe my thinking is lined up with the Word of God because the greater One lives inside of me. I declare my thoughts are filled with *whatsoever things are true, honest, just, lovely, of a good report, and whatsoever is worthy of praise* (Philippians 4:8)! I thank you, Heavenly Father, my heart and mind are filled with your peace as I wait patiently for you. Amen!

Waiting for God

I've never met anyone who truly enjoys a long season of waiting. But, when we wait on God, there are so many benefits that come to us while we wait. None of us like to go through the process of waiting because we live in a microwave society, which tells us everything we want must be given to us right on the spot. When was the last time you had to stand in a long line? How many times did you complain, or how many times did you hear someone else standing in the line calling for the manager? Most believers believe that waiting for God means to sit around and do absolutely nothing. But, I believe God wants us to seek Him until He is found. Seeking God is not just sitting around and waiting for something to drop in your lap.

But, the Bible tells us, "But they that wait upon the LORD shall renew their strength; they shall mount up with wings as eagles; they shall run and not be weary, and they shall walk and not faint" (Isaiah 40:31 KJV). The word *wait* in this verse according to the Hebrew dictionary is *Kaw-vaw*. It means "to look for," "hope," and "expect." The believer must take on the position of looking for, hoping, and expecting God to move on his or her behalf. While a believer is in a season of waiting, we must spend time in the secret place of God, so we can find rest. Rest is found in God. We must rest completely in the finished work of the cross and trust that everything we could possibly need has already been given to us. Once we rest in God, our strength is renewed, and only then are we able to depend, trust, and expect God to move. There are so many spiritual benefits a believer can gain when he or she remains in expectation on God to move. Expectation teaches us patience, endurance, confidence, and assurance in God. It instructs us on how to be faithful to God, and it help us to keep hope alive.

The Word of God clearly states, *there is a time and season for everything* (Ecclesiastes 3:1-8). However, faith causes time to move, and when we step out in faith, faith allows us to cross over to the supernatural, and time is no longer of the essence. But, don't forget, the Bible says, *The promises of God are inherited through faith and patience* according to Hebrews 6:12. There is no way of separating the two. If someone says they have faith, then the fruit of patience will be exhibited in his or her life. Faith and patience go hand in hand.

Confession While Waiting for God

Jehovah, I thank you for renewing my strength while I wait for you. I know you, Jehovah Shammah, are here with me and *even the youths shall faint and get weary, but I declare I will not, I am soaring on wings like eagles* (Isaiah 40:30-31). *My soul waits for the LORD, and in His Word, I find hope* (Psalm 130:5). I thank you, Master, my hope is in you alone, and right now, I take your supernatural strength by faith, *(Speak in the Holy Spirit or clap your hands)*, as I walk through this season of waiting. I declare and decree I will not lose heart, and I will not become discouraged, exhausted, and wearied through fear. I will trust you, LORD, and I will not *lean on my own understanding, but in all I do I will acknowledge you and thank you Lord for directing my path* (Proverbs 3:6). While I wait, *my inner man is being renewed each day* as I go through this period of waiting (II Corinthians 4:16). So, teach me, LORD, how to remain steadfast in your presence while I am waiting to see manifestation come to pass in my life *(Speak in the Holy Spirit or clap your hands)*. Help me, LORD, not to *get tired of doing what's good because in due time, I will reap a harvest if I do not give up* (Galatians 6:9). I worship you in advance Father, and I praise you because your Word says, *No good thing will you withhold from those who walk upright before you* (Psalm 84:11), and *if I draw nigh to you, you will draw nigh to me (James 4:8)*. Teach me how to remain quiet in this position of rest, waiting, and expecting you to answer me. Father, your Word says *those who wait on you will inherit the earth* (Psalm 37:9), and I believe I will not be put to shame or be disappointed in Jesus' name. *(Speak in the Holy Spirit or clap your hands)*. I receive my answer now through your Word, a vision, a dream, your voice, through a spoken word, or through the mouth of someone who knows your voice. Thank you, El Shaddai, that my steps are made clear, and you have ordered my steps in your Word. So, right now I commit myself to your keeping and your plan while I wait patiently for you. Amen!

Breaking Free from an Unforgiving Heart

Unforgiveness is a blessing blocker. It is a hindrance in the life of a born-again believer. The past, present, and future sins of the believer have already been forgiven. Thus, because we received forgiveness free of charge at the time of salvation, this truth should enable us to forgive others. But, this is not always the case. Many believers carry around unforgiveness toward other people for years. Sadly, some of the people who have offended them or misused them are dead, but they are still holding on to bitterness and have some resentful feelings toward them. Unforgiveness is not only a blessing blocker, but it hinders the believer's prayer life. The Bible says, "Whenever you stand praying, if you have anything against anyone, forgive him [drop the issue, let it go], so that your Father who is in heaven will also forgive you your transgressions and wrongdoings [against Him and others]" (Mark 11:25 (AMP). When a believer walks around in unforgiveness, the prayers of the individual are not heard by God.

Moreover, unforgiveness not only hinders the believer's prayer life, but it opens doors for demonic spirits in their lives that manifest themselves through sickness and disease. The Word of God tells us in Ephesians 4:31-32 (KJV), "Let all bitterness, and wrath, and anger, and clamor, and evil speaking, be put away from you, with all malice: And be ye kind one to another, tenderhearted, forgiving one another, even as God for Christ's sake hath forgiven you." We must live free from unforgiveness because it opens the door to pain in our lives.

I encountered one woman of God who came to me for prayer. When she began to explain to me why she needed prayer, my heart was broken for her. She told me she had about seven surgeries. She said, "Sister Maxine, every time they fixed something, something else kept popping up." Also, this woman of God had about five different diseases in her body. It was painful to listen to her, not because I thought the diseases were bigger than Jehovah Rapha, but because I could hear it in her voice: she was exhausted. She was tired of dealing with it. I felt tears beginning to roll down my face because I felt compassion and love manifesting through me like a force. I knew God was able, so I started to pray.

I called on Jehovah Rapha because I know He still heals. While I was praying, the Holy Spirit said to me to ask her if she was holding unforgiveness in her heart. I thought for a minute, *Lord what does this have to do with healing*? Then, I took a deep breath and stepped out on faith and said, "Can I ask you a question?" "Do you have any unforgiveness in your heart?" She said, "I have to be honest. When anyone does anything bad to me, I cut them out! In fact, my children's father offended me years ago, and I took my children and left. I haven't talked to him since, and this was years ago." My heart was aching even more because she had not realized that because of her unforgiving heart, sickness and disease had made a home in her body.

This woman of God needed an encounter with true love in order to walk in constant forgiveness. One taste of the real love of God would change her life forever. So, I told her God loved her so much, and I prayed that God would give her the courage to let go of her offenses, so she could receive her healing. Forgiveness is for us, and it is a powerful weapon against the enemy. If we don't forgive others, then that person keeps us in prison. One of the most significant examples of forgiveness we see is in the life of Jesus. The Pharisees and Sadducees agreed on one thing—that Jesus had to die, even though they couldn't find any fault in Him. Knowing that purpose had to be fulfilled, Jesus still cried out on the cross, "Father, forgive them; for they know not what they do" (Luke 23:34 KJV).

Confession for Breaking Free from an Unforgiving Heart

I cry out to you, my Savior and Lord, because I admit there is unforgiveness in my heart toward (fill in the name(s) here). But, your Word says *when I stand praying, first forgive anyone I am holding a grudge against, so that my father in heaven will forgive me* (Mark 11:25), and you shall save me, and rescue me from danger or destruction. Therefore, I renounce and let go of the spirit of unforgiveness that has plagued my life! *(Speak in the Holy Spirit or clap your hands).* Your Word declares *if I forgive men of their sins, you, Father, will also forgive me of my sins* (Matthew 6:15). So, I empty my hurts at your feet, and I let go of my offense and the pain of my past. I let go of all the wrong (fill in the name(s) here) have done toward my family and me *(Speak in the Holy Spirit or clap your hands)*.

I let go of every harsh word that has been said wrongfully against my name. I forgive (fill in the name(s) here) of the abuse, shame, offense, and pain, and today, I choose to give up my hurt because I know it's your will. I repent for the offense I have been holding on to that has caused me to walk contrary to your Word. But, today, I believe I'm well on my way to take the first step, and I surrender myself at your feet. I speak to every lousy seed that was spoken over my life. I curse every evil word spoken to me or against my children, and I stand in my authority, and I command *it* to *die* in Jesus' name. I denounce and curse every demonic decree, open portal of evil, and assignments that have been assigned to my life and to my seed, and I command you to catch fire *(Speak in the Holy Spirit or clap your hands)*.

I denounce the spirits of pride, bitterness, anger, and strife that have been plaguing my life. I command you to leave me now, and I surrender my life to Jesus. I thank you, LORD, in advance that you have already healed my broken heart and restored my crushed spirit. Thank you, Adonai! I believe the spirit of unforgiveness has left me, and I believe I am free by the blood of Jesus. I receive the freedom Jesus has given me right now! Amen!

Remaining Consistent During Testing

We all know the story of Job; He went through a season of great testing. He lost everything he held so dearly to his heart because God knew Job was faithful, and he was a man of integrity. But, Job walked in fear, and what he feared most became a reality in his life. During Job's time of testing, he had many distractions. His friends accused him of sinning against God because of how Job's situation looked in the natural (Job, chapters 8-22).

Nevertheless, the Bible says, "Beloved, think it not strange concerning the fiery trial which is to try you, as though some strange thing happened unto you: But rejoice, inasmuch as ye are partakers of Christ's sufferings; that, when his glory shall be revealed, ye may be glad also with exceeding joy" (I Peter 4:12-13 KJV). The next time the enemy tells you trials are not the will of God, tell him just as in the case of Job, it will work for your good. Tell him there is absolutely nothing that happens in your life that takes God by surprise. Here is some more good news. If you are going through a season of testing, every trial you find yourself in, God has already made *a way for you to escape, and He will not let you be tempted beyond what you can handle* (I Corinthians 10:13).

God has already set in motion an expiration date for every trouble that we could ever face, and you can start now by giving Him glory! He has already made a way out of it. It is not possible to be a believer and not go through testing. We see a great example in the life of Abraham. First, God told Abraham to leave his father and mother and go to a land he was unfamiliar with in Genesis 12:1. Abraham trusted and obeyed God. He did what God said. Then, Abraham was told to send Hagar and Ishmael away (Genesis 21:8-21). Can you imagine the pain Abraham felt as a result of sending his firstborn away? If that wasn't enough, when Isaac—the son of promise was born, Abraham endured another test. God told Abraham to take Isaac and sacrifice him on Mount Moriah (Genesis 22:1-19). Again, because Abraham trusted God and had committed himself to God, I believe Isaac was already dead in the mind of Abraham, as he made his way up to Mount Moriah.

We see, during Abraham's period of testing, he does not waver in his belief toward God. Even when it looked impossible, he still walked in obedience to the will of God. In the same way, when believers are going through a time of testing, we must delight ourselves in the Word of God, and whatever we are facing, stay faithful trusting God, and wait patiently for His instructions. Also, believers must resist all distractions that come our way and keep our eyes on God, even if people around us are speaking contrary. Hearing the voice of God is critical at this time because one instruction from God will change our lives. Believers also should *never* focus on the problem because if we keep our eyes focused on the issue, we will find ourselves overpowered by the cares of life. During a time of testing, reading and confessing the Word is essential because the Bible says, *He will watch over His word and bring it to pass* (Jeremiah 1:12). Also, being thankful is a vehicle that helps us enter a place of rest while waiting on God's manifestation.

Confession During Times of Testing

I decree and declare this *is the day the Lord has made*. I'm choosing to *rejoice and be exceedingly glad in it* name of Jesus, I declare, and therefore, I will speak. Father, I thank you right now that *I walk by faith and not by sight* (II Corinthians 5:7), and I decree my trust is in you alone. I believe, Father, you will not put more on me than what I can handle. I commit myself to your keeping, and during this difficult and trying season of my life, I believe I am blood-bought, Holy Ghost-filled, chosen by God, and I am an overcomer. I declare victory over defeat in every situation that is trying to keep me from moving forward *(Speak in the Holy Spirit or clap your hands)*.

Father, your Word says that *whosoever is born of God has already overcome the world* (I John 5:4), and right now I stand in my authority, and I declare I have already overcome. I choose to *count it all joy,* and as I walk through this time of testing, I know that my faith is producing endurance (James 1:1-2). I decree and declare that before this trial is over, perseverance and the fruit of patience will have a chance to grow, and I believe I am *perfect and complete, lacking nothing* (James 1:4). Jehovah Shalom, you are my peace, and right now I rest in your unchanging hands *(Speak in the Holy Spirit or clap your hands)*. I sing praises and glory to you, Father, because you alone are worthy of all my praise. I am resting in the secret place where I am protected, and I'm at peace.

Teach me, Lord, how to lean on you and acknowledge you in everything I do. Baptize me with the spirit of prayer and teach me how to pray and intercede on behalf of the lost. Open my eyes that I may see new revelation in your Word. Thank you, Father, for keeping me from falling. I present myself faultless by faith to you. I declare and decree my season of change is now, and *my latter will be greater than my former* according to Haggai 2:9! I say thanks in advance for what you have already done in Jesus' name. Amen!

When my Enemies Rise up Against me

The Bible says that *without love, our faith doesn't work* (Galatians 5:6). So love should be the ultimate goal when our enemies rise up against us. It takes the love of God and maturity in God to love those who hate us. Mature Christians take time to renew their minds in the Word of God. Also, they accept and see people the same way God sees them. I believe one way we can identify a mature believer is by how they treat their enemies and by their fruit. When a believer is mature, the "fruit of the spirit" will manifest through their lives. These "fruits of the spirit" are the character of God. When the fruit is cultivated, believers will easily demonstrate who God is through their lives.

So, the minute our enemies rise against us, the response of a mature believer will be love. God has instructed us to love our enemies because He loved those who spat, lied, beat, and accused Him of wrongdoing. The world loves people who love them, but they turn their backs on those who are their enemies. Loving our enemies requires submitting to God's Word, dying to flesh, and allowing God's will to be done in our lives. Once believers die to self, they lay his or her will at the feet of Jesus and delight themselves in His will. The minute our enemies rise up against us, our responsibility is to delight ourselves in the promises of God and allow His Word to manifest in our lives. Then, He will fight every battle against our enemies. Jesus, the High Priest, is LORD behind every confession; therefore, our ultimate position when the enemy attacks us is to find rest by confessing and declaring the Word of God. We should keep in mind that Satan is the one who has launched an attack against us, not the person, even though it appears to be so. When we delight ourselves in the Word of God, we position ourselves to allow God to fight for us. The *battle is not ours, but it belongs to the LORD* (II Chronicles 20:15).

Confession for When my Enemies Rise up Against Me

Heavenly Father, I thank you for being the lifter of my head, and your Word says, *When the enemy comes in like a flood, your spirit will lift up a standard, and I command a standard to be lifted up against my enemies* (Isaiah 59:19). I stand in my authority that Jesus has given me, and I cancel every plot or plan Satan has established by using human beings as an instrument to disturb the peace Jesus has given me (*Pray in the Holy Spirit or clap your hands*). I command every assignment the enemy has sent out against me to be destroyed; I curse it right now in the name of Jesus. I decree and declare *no weapon that has been formed against me will prosper, and every tongue that rises up against me in judgment will be condemned* (Isaiah 54:17), and everyone who has dug a grave for me, he will fall into it himself.

I command the spirit of sabotage to die by fire, and I speak to every spirit of revenge, and I command you to go back to the sender right now *(Pray in the Holy Spirit or clap your hands)*. Every plan that has been sent out to frustrate me by trying to hinder the plans of God from going forth, I bind you right now! The Lord rebuke you, and I decree and declare that my enemies which have risen up against me, be smitten before my face. *They may be coming against me one way, but I command them to flee seven ways* (Deuteronomy 28:7).

Thank you, Jehovah Rohi. You are my Shepherd, *and you have already prepared a table for me in the presence of my enemies* (Psalm 23:5). Almighty and eternal Father, I ask you to save my enemies. Send a laborer in your vineyard to minister the good news to them! I command their spiritual eyes and ears to be opened, and the veil that is over their minds to be lifted *(Pray in the Holy Spirit or clap your hands)*. Thank you, Father, they are saved, their minds are renewed in your Word, and their eyes are opened to the truth. I decree and declare *my enemies are my footstool* (Psalm 110:1), and they *are at peace with me* according to Proverbs 16:7, in Jesus' name. Amen!

Walking through Seasons of Uncertainty

Delay is not a denial! Are you going through a season of uncertainty in your life? Can you say you have no idea what to do next or where to go? I can relate to how you are feeling. There were seasons in my life where I had no idea what my next move was. I felt completely hopeless. Even though I knew God was with me, and I was not alone, I felt like I did not know what to do next. I also felt as though God had forgotten about me because it was difficult to hear His voice. During this season of my life, I felt vagueness and fear creep in because the devil was telling me I was going to be homeless. My husband went from being on active duty to being discharged within a week, and our lives changed that quickly. We went from being employed to unemployed. Maybe, for you, it's not employment; perhaps, it's a relationship, death of a loved one, or your own business.

IF YOU CHANGE YOUR WORDS,
YOU'LL CHANGE YOUR LIFE!

If this is where you are right now, you are not alone. The Word of God says, *He will never leave you nor forsake you. He is with you until the end of the earth* (Hebrews 13:5). I know it is difficult right now, and you have no idea what to do next or where to go. But, during this season of uncertainty, I want to tell you *God knows the plans and thoughts He thinks towards you. They are thoughts of good and not evil—to take you to your expected end* according to Jeremiah 29:11. Even though it's difficult, get into the position of praying and fasting—seek the face of God until He reveals your next step. In this position, you will receive supernatural strength to wait patiently for God.

Stay in the posture of faith, then walk in expectation to receive instruction for your next move. When we are going through a season of uncertainty, it is vital not to make any decisions without hearing the voice of God. The spirit of confusion may try to creep in to confuse you and take you off track. This is why fasting and praying is critical during this time. Also, the spirit of fear may enter into your hearts if you don't guard your hearts. So, be careful. The Bible tells us, *Whatsoever you think in your heart* (Hebrew word is *nephesh*, which means: mind, soul, desire, inner being of the man and emotion), *so are you* (Proverbs 23:7). If fear comes, destroy it with the Word of God because *God has not given you the spirit of fear, but God has given us a spirit of power, love, and a sound mind* (II Timothy 1:7).

Did you carry out the last instruction that God gave you? The reason I am asking this question is because God will never give believers all the steps at once. He will provide us with one step at a time. So, if you did not follow God's last instruction, you are not waiting for God; God is waiting on you. If you did follow God's last instruction, then it is time to rest in God's plan for you. Know that God is faithful! Sit yourself down in His Word and wait patiently for Him. He will not disappoint you!

Confession for Rest in Times of Uncertainty

Father, in the name of Jesus, I cut off all second heaven activities right now that would try to prevent this prayer from reaching the third heaven *(Pray in the Holy Spirit or clap your hands)*. I bind every diabolical spirit that has been assigned to my life and the lives of my family *(Speak in the Holy Spirit and clap your hands)*. I dispatch Michael, the archangel of God, to go and fight and clear away every satanic and demonic interference over this atmosphere now *(Pray in the Holy Spirit or clap your hands)*.

Jehovah Shammah, I know I am not alone because your Word says, *you will never leave me nor forsake me (Deuteronomy 31:6).* Father, I declare and decree that, because I believe, I enter into your rest. I rest in the finished work of the cross, and I know everything I need has already been given to me before the foundation of this earth. So, right now, I declare and decree all is well by faith! I will not be anxious about anything, but in every situation, *with prayer and supplication, I am making my requests known to you* according to Philippians 4:6. (Pray and tell God what you need here). I ask that your *will be done in my life as it is in heaven* (Matthew 6:10). During this time of uncertainty, I thank you for your peace, *which passes all understanding* (Philippians 4:7).

Thank you that my heart and mind are in your rest. I decree and declare victory, restoration, and breakthrough in my life. I decree the spirits of fear, worry, doubt, unbelief, and limitations have been broken, and I am free *(Speak in the Holy Spirit and clap your hands)*. Satan's power has been broken, and I command my heart to settle down and receive the peace God has given me through His son. I call forth the wisdom of God, and I command the wisdom and favor of God to manifest in my life now. I thank you, Lord, and I fix my mind on things *that are true, honest, just, pure, lovely and of a good report* (Philippians 4:8). Amen! Now, walk in expectation to see manifestation of your prayer come to pass in your life!

Children

The Word of the Lord declares *that believers must train up their children in the way they should go, and when they are old, they shall not depart from it* (Proverbs 22:6). Most believers I know did take the time to impart the Word of God into the lives of their children. However, for some children, when they are old enough to make decisions on their own, some of them walk away from their faith for a season. I know this from experience. I grew up in church, but when I was old enough to make my own decision, I walked away from God for a season in my life. I went through a lot of pain during this season, and when I finally rededicated my heart back to the Lord, fear crept into my heart concerning my children. I did not want them to go through what I had gone through in life, so I became very overprotective concerning them. God began to show me, little by little, that He had them in the palm of His hands, and because I had trained them up in His ways, the teaching and the seed that had been planted in them would grow into a plant. So, even though it seems like they are walking contrary to His Word, they will return to their foundation, which has already been laid on the inside of them. This season is only for a short time.

Faith-based confessions over the lives of our children are essential. God's Word must take first place in their lives. If the believer only speaks what he or she see and hear about their children, their words will become a reality. We must say *only* what God says about our children, even during difficult times because, "Death and life are in the power of the tongue, and they that love it shall eat the fruit thereof" (Proverbs 18:21 KJV). What will you speak in difficult times—life or death? The Bible says *the seed of the righteous will be delivered* (Proverbs 11:21). So, it doesn't matter what it looks like today. *Believe God's Word!*

When my son reached eighteen, it seemed like he just turned into this different person overnight. We had been having some miscommunication. One day during a heated discussion, he moved out and went to live with his girlfriend. During this tough time, God began showing me my son needed his testimony, and that if I loved him more than God loved him, I

CHILDREN

would lose him. So, one morning, with tears in my eyes, I released him to God. During this time, I drew closer to God in prayer for my son's safe return home. Three weeks passed, and he still hadn't come back. I felt led to go on seven days of fasting and praying. I stood on the Word, confessing it over him every morning. On the seventh day of the fast, something happened. I received a notification in the mail that he had changed his address. Then, I heard the devil saying, "Look at you. Your fasting didn't work." I called him a liar and told him that if my grandmothers' fasting and prayer got results, so can I. After that, I wept in prayer until I fell asleep. The very next day, I realized the enemy was trying to steal my breakthrough. My son came home, and my prayers were answered!

I found out while my son was away that God had placed him in the company of a woman of God who spoke into his life. Because she did, God opened his eyes. He said he recognized he had good parents, and he needed to come home. I shared this testimony to let you know that it does not matter what it looks like in the life of your child or children right now. God is no respecter of persons (Romans 2:11). Maybe your child is in prison, is battling with an addiction, or has even walked away from God. Don't give up! If God brought my child home, he will do the same thing for you. He is well able to deliver your child. *Do not get tired of doing what is good because in due season you will reap if you don't give up* (Galatians 6:9).

Confession Over Children

Father, today, your Word is true, and I believe it and make it final in my children's lives. I believe in my heart and declare with my mouth that your Word will prevail over (say children's names here) lives. According to Joel 2:28, you say *you will pour out your spirit upon my sons and my daughters.* So I believe they are saved, and your spirit that is living on the inside of them is the final authority in their lives *(Speak in the Holy Spirit and clap your hands).* I declare and decree that (say children's names here) *are taught of the Lord, and great is their peace* (Isaiah 54:13). I believe my children/grandchildren are wise. They take heed to godly instruction, correction, and the wisdom of God is their portion. I declare and decree they are filled with the Holy Spirit; they know who they are in Christ Jesus, and their minds are renewed in your Word.

Covenant-keeping God, I thank you right now that they are in your keeping, and their hands are pure from evil, and you are keeping their feet on the path of righteousness *(Speak in the Holy Spirit and clap your hands)*. I am not moved by what I see, hear, and what appears to be in their lives. I declare and decree everywhere their feet tread, I release ministering angels to go before them, protect and take charge over them in Jesus' name. I declare and decree a *thousand shall fall on their side and ten thousand shall fall on their right, but no evil shall come near them, and only with their eyes shall they see the reward of the wicked* (Psalm 91:7) *(Speak in the Holy Spirit and clap your hands)*. I believe my work shall be rewarded, and my children will come home from the land of the enemy as God has promised (Jeremiah 31:16). I call (say children's names here) home *now* in Jesus' name!

I apply the blood of Jesus over (say children's names here), and I declare he/she/they *are the head and not the tail; they are the lender and not the borrower, above and not at the bottom* (Deuteronomy 28:12). I declare and decree they are *increasing in wisdom and in stature and in favor with you and with men* (Luke 2:52). I commit them to your keeping, Father, and I know *you have begun a good work in their lives, and you are faithful to bring every promise to pass* in their lives (Philippians 1:6). Thank you, LORD, for perfecting that which concerns me in Jesus' name. Amen!

Confessions for Adult Children

Father, I believe and confess right now by faith that (say adult children's names) are your disciples, taught of you, and they walk in total obedience to your Word. I decree and declare they are wise because they accept godly wisdom and instruction according to your Word. Father, because I have obeyed your Word and trained them up in your Word, I am not moved by what I see, hear, or feel about their lives. Father, wherever (say adult children's names) is right *now*, I have full confidence and trust in you that angels are watching over (him/her/them), and no harm shall come near (say adult children's names) *(Speak in the Holy Spirit and clap your hands)*.

I decree and declare by faith that you have already prepared a godly spouse for (say adult children's names), and that they are a man or woman of God after your own heart. I release deliverance over the lives of (say adult children's names). I come against all *principalities, powers, rulers of the darkness of this world, and every spiritual wickedness in high places*, (Ephesians

6:12) that is in operation in the lives of my children *(Speak in the Holy Spirit and clap your hands)*. Wherever they may be right now, I decree and declare that every chain and hindering spirit is broken off their lives *now*! I break every addiction to alcohol, drugs, sex, love of money, and the spirit of lust in his or her lives, in the name of Jesus *(Speak in the Holy Spirit and clap your hands)*. I speak to every satanic and demonic spirit in operation in the lives of (say adult children's names) *(Speak in the Holy Spirit and clap your hands)*. I release fire, fire, fire to burn your plan in the lives of (say adult children's names) *(Speak in the Holy Spirit and clap your hands)*. Satan, the Lord rebuke your assignment in the lives of my children. I thank you, LORD, that (say adult children's names) spiritual ears, eyes, and minds are *being enlightened; that they will know what is the hope of their calling in Christ Jesus* (Ephesians 1:18). I declare and decree that everywhere their feet touch today, the blessings of the LORD are over them *(Speak in the Holy Spirit and clap your hands)*. I pray that you will bless and keep (say adult children's names) *and make your face to shine upon them and be gracious to them.* I pray that you *lift up your countenance on them and give them your peace* (Numbers 6:24-26) *(Pray in the Holy Spirit and clap your hands)*. I release the perfect will of God over my children' lives now in Jesus' name. Amen!

A Marriage Made in Heaven

When I think about marriage in the kingdom of God, I think about Christ's expression of love for His bride, the church. God did not want the first man, Adam, to be alone, so He created Eve to be his helpmate and companion. God called Adam and Eve, Adam in Genesis 5:2, which signifies their oneness. This is an indication of the binding covenant God established between a man and a woman. So, our spouse is a gift from God to us. Therefore, the Bible says, *a man shall leave his father and mother and be joined to his wife, and they shall be one* flesh (Genesis 2:24). The man and woman are forsaking their own parents and clinging to each other to become one flesh.

Marriage is an expression of God's love for humanity. This binding covenant is a *threefold cord that is not easily broken* (Ecclesiastes 4:12), and it lasts until death. The woman submits herself to her husband, *and the man loves his wife as Christ loved the church and gave himself for it* (Ephesians 5:22, 25). God did not create marriage to be a business; neither did He create marriage to be between a man and a man, or a woman and a woman. That is an abomination unto God. Furthermore, the Word of God tells believers to not be unequally yoked together with unbelievers *because two people can't walk together if they do not agree*, according to Amos 3:3. When God blesses us with a spouse, this blessing *will make us rich and adds no sorrow to it* (Proverbs 10:22). God's blessings are supposed to enrich us and move us to another level. I have some good news for you today—even if you marry someone outside of God's will, God can still turn your marriage around for His glory. He can turn your mess into a message. Even if your marriage is on the verge of a divorce, or you may be separated right now, there is still hope.

I heard one woman's amazing testimony. She had been separated from her husband for ten years. She used her faith in the Word and sowed a seed toward her broken marriage. She then walked around confessing, "I have my husband back, and I am pregnant with his child." After ten years of being separated from her husband, this woman of God got exactly what she decreed. She was reconciled with her husband, and she became pregnant! The Bible says, the Word of God is spirit and it is life (John 6:63), so you must make a decision right now to fight for your marriage. This is done by adding works to your faith by standing on Word-based confessions daily. In spite of what it looks like in your marriage, keep your faith in the Word of God, and you will have what you say.

Confession for a Marriage Made in Heaven

I declare and decree my marriage is made in heaven, *and no weapon that has been formed against my marriage will prosper; and every tongue that rises up against my marriage be condemned according to* Isaiah 54:17. *(Speak in the Holy Spirit and clap your hands).* I believe we share our deepest secrets with each other, and we open ourselves and invite each other in. I confess I have no secrets my spouse does not know. I believe my marriage is fruitful because I live and walk in obedience to the Word of God, and I choose to commit myself to do what the Word of God says concerning my marriage. God has placed us together, and no man, not even me, will separate or divide us.

(Speak in the Holy Spirit and clap your hands). I ask you right now, Father, to give my spouse the ability to hear your voice and respond to convictions. I decree that he/she will not look lustfully at a man or a woman, and I intercept every plan of the enemy against (say your spouse's name here) in Jesus' name. I plead the blood of Jesus over his/her eyes, and I uproot every lustful desire or thought that is

trying to take root in his/her heart *(Speak in the Holy Spirit and clap your hands)*. I decree that, today, we are falling in love with each other all over again. I declare and decree I find no fault or wrong in (say your spouse's name here), and I see him/her the way God sees him/her. I declare and decree *we are not self-seeking, rude, proud, boastful nor jealous; but we are loving, kind, patient,* and we put each other's interests and needs before our own needs (I Corinthians 13:4-5). I declare and decree our marriage is the *threefold cord that is not easily broken* according to Ecclesiastes 4:12, with God at the center.

I break the hold over his/her life of every generational curse, soul tie, and unsettled issue, and I cut off every third party because God has put us together, and no one will separate us. I bind the spirit of Jezebel and every evil spirit that is trying to divide our marriage in the name of Jesus. I speak over every part of my marriage that is dead. I speak resurrection power and life over it right now *(Speak in the Holy Spirit and clap your hands)*. I declare that Jesus is LORD over our finances, communication, health, commitment, sexual intimacy, children, purpose, ministry, and business. I declare and decree *we are quick to listen, slow to speak, and slow to get angry* with each other, our children, and anyone we come in contact with in Jesus' name according to James 1:19. Amen!

Desiring to be Married

If you have been waiting a long time to get married, I am here to tell you to wait no longer. I declare and decree this is the year you will get married, in Jesus' name! The Bible says in Hebrews 10:38 *that the just shall live by faith*. In *Strong's Exhaustive Concordance of the Bible*, the Greek word for faith is *pistis*. Pistis means believe, assurance, or belief. So, in other words, the just shall live by believing in the finished work of the cross. In the kingdom, we take what we have asked for before we can see manifestation with our naked eyes. Faith is believing in what has already been made available to us in the invisible world and transferring those things from the invisible to the visible world around us. Faith lives outside of our five senses and is based on the reality of the Word of God. According to Mark 11:24, we *can pray for anything, and if you believe that you've received it, it will be yours.* Faith is now, and hope is for the future, according to Hebrews 11:1. Everything we need has already been given to us for life and godly living (II Peter 1:3). So, we must reach out by faith (believing) and take possession of everything that has already been made available for us in the supernatural.

Here is a personal testimony of my own from nearly eighteen years ago. My sister called and told me she was getting married. By faith, I opened my mouth and said, "I am going to come to your wedding with my husband." Please note, I was not even dating anyone, nor did I have anyone in mind. These words of faith just came out of my mouth without a single thought! When my sister heard these words, she laughed. She wanted to know how that was going to be possible if I wasn't even dating anybody, and the wedding was about eight months away. I had no idea how, but I stepped my foot in the supernatural and brought the future into my now. I did not have an answer for her, but I knew words would create what I desired.

After this, I did not go looking, nor did I allow unbelief to step in. I rested in God, and my sister got married that following September of the next year. What I had confessed became a reality. My husband accompanied me to my sister's wedding. So, faith is a bridge to the supernatural; it makes everything that is impossible, possible.

God had you read this book so I could encourage you to put your faith in the now. God is not going to do it; He has already done it. Right now, by faith, open your mouth and declare, "This is the year I will get married!" Call a friend now and say by faith, "This is the year I will get married!" Before we go on to the confession, I have to warn you; the devil heard that confession, so make sure you say, "No," when a counterfeit comes. The enemy will probably send an imitation before the real thing!

Now, let me explain to you what spiritual husbands and wives are. These are demonic spirits who marry or have sexual intercourse with a woman or a man during the night. By doing so, they connect themselves to the individual spiritually, so they will either not get married, or never have a successful relationship. If you are battling with these spirits at night, you need deliverance. Also, check for any generational curses you need to denounce concerning relationships. Then, you'll be on your way to freedom. Get yourself ready. I hear wedding bells ringing!

Confession for Desiring to Get Married

I declare and decree right now that this is the year I will marry the man/woman of mydreams. I believe *life and death are in the power of my tongue* (Proverbs 18:21), and I choose to speak life. I confess my husband/wife shall find me and before the close of this year, we will become one flesh. The Word of God says, *If I delight myself in the Lord, He will give me my heart's desire* (Psalm 37:4). Right now, I commit myself in the ways of the LORD, and I believe it has already come to pass in the name of Jesus. All my trust is in you, LORD, and I rely on you because I believe you know what is best for me. I break and renounce every evil covenant that has been assigned to my life from my mother's house and my father's house preventing me from getting married or having a successful relationship. I release fire, fire, fire to burn every ancestral covenant in Jesus' name *(Speak in the Holy Spirit and clap your hands)*. I bind every plot or plan that has been binding me spiritually and hindering me from moving forward in marriage, and I call the enemy's works powerless and declare and decree they have no power over me in the name of Jesus!

I denounce every *husband or wife spirit* that has been assigned to my bloodline and has been handed down from my ancestors, to be cursed. I loose myself from your assignments, and I break loose from every evil relationship. I release fire, fire, fire in the name of Jesus (*Speak in the Holy Spirit and clap your hands*). I believe Christ *has redeemed me from the curse of the law, and He was made a curse for me. For it is written, cursed is every one that hang on a tree* (Galatians 3:13). I speak to the spirit of delay, and I command you to catch on fire now *(Speak in the Holy Spirit and clap your hands).* I cut the cord of every ungodly soul-tie from past relationships, and I command you to die from your roots. Father, open my eyes to see clearly when the enemy tries to trap me with a counterfeit husband/wife. *Lead me not into temptation but deliver me from all evil* (Matthew 6:13). Heavenly Father, give me the desire to keep pursuing purity and rest in your appointed time. Thank you for the courage to say, "No," when temptation comes my way. I call forth my godly husband/wife. I command you to *manifest* yourself right now because it is not the will of God, I should be alone. I believe I receive everything I ask in Jesus' name. Amen!

Overcoming Temptation

If you are living and breathing, I have some news for you. The evil one has access to tempt you, whether you like it or not. Being tempted is not a sin, but what you do when temptation comes your way matter the most. *Jesus was led by the Spirit up to the mountain to be tempted by Satan* (Matthew 4:1). He overcame His temptation because He had the Word and spirit; He came out victorious, and so can we. We should follow His example when we are tempted. Jesus never sinned when He was tempted. He spoke the Word of God boldly to Satan. I believe we are tempted the most when we are under great physical or emotional stress, and when we are getting ready to be promoted. Also, temptation comes when we are lonely, going through uncertainties, under pressure, tired, confused, lack identity, and many other reasons. The minute we find ourselves in these awkward positions of temptation, we must remember

Jesus went through the same trials, and if He overcame temptation, so can we. The Word of God says, *As Jesus is so are we in this world* (I John 4:17). Likewise, *when our temptation is great, we should look for the way out, that God has provided* (I Corinthians 10:13).

Hence, if you're going through a season of temptation, open your eyes and look for the way God has already made available for you. Ask God to open your eyes to see the way out, resist the devil, and look for the escape route. The Word of God tells us, "So submit to [the authority of] God. Resist the devil [stand firm against him], and he will flee from you" (James 4:7 AMP). We must pray for God's strength to resist and turn away from all temptation. We have another great example in the Word of God that teaches us how to deal with temptation. When Potiphar's wife tried to seduce Joseph, he bolted away from the scene, leaving behind a piece of his garment (Genesis 39:12-14). We should also run for our lives, without looking back. Satan might have access to tempt you, but God won't allow you to be tempted beyond what you can handle. Thank you, Jesus!

Confession in the Time of Temptation

Father, in the name of Jesus, I decree and declare according to I Corinthians 10:13, there is no temptation so great that *you haven't already made a way for me to escape* (*Speak in the Holy Spirit and clap your hands*). Your Word declares I am blessed because, if I endure temptation, *I shall receive the crown of life,* which you promised to me because I love you according to James 1:12. Therefore, Father, I receive your supernatural strength to overcome this period of temptation and to come out on top. I believe and declare right now, *I can do all things because you have given me the strength,* according to Philippians 4:13. So, I command my will, emotions, and every thought to submit itself to your Word *(Speak in the Holy Spirit and clap your hands)*. I submit myself to God, and I command you, Satan, to flee in the name of Jesus. I take every evil imagination captive, and I surrender myself to Jesus.

I plead the blood of Jesus over my mind, and I intercept every plot and plan of the enemy over my mind. I saturate myself with the blood of Jesus, and I command every trap the enemy has set up for me to be exposed and come to nothing in Jesus' name. The angels of God have charge over me, and I choose right now to walk in full obedience to the Word of God. I say, "No" to the temptation of (say whatever temptations you are facing). I resist you, destroy your plans, and release fire over every assignment of the evil one *(Speak in the Holy Spirit and clap your hands)*. Every trap the enemy has sent out against me, I command it to backfire and go back to the sender in Jesus' name.

Father, your Word declares *if I keep my mind on you, you will keep me in perfect peace* (Isaiah 26:3). I declare and decree I am walking in your peace, and I abide in you, and your Word abides in me. I ask you to open my eyes to see my way of escape (John 15:7). I ask you to hide me under your feathers and deliver me from all evil in the name of Jesus! *(Speak in the Holy Spirit and clap your hands)*. Thank you, Lord, for the strength to remain patient in tribulation and constant in prayer during this period of my life, in Jesus' name! Amen.

Overcoming the Spirit of Fear

Fear is a demonic spirit, and it is a weapon Satan uses against believers. Every human being will deal with fear at some point or another, but what we do when it comes makes the difference. The Word of God says in I John 4:18 (KJV), "There is no fear in love; but perfect love casteth out fear: because fear hath torment. He that feareth is not made perfect in love." Fear has punishment, but God's love for us is perfect and complete, needing nothing. His love for us gives us perfect peace. So, if we allow fear to torment us, the love of God does not richly dwell in our hearts.

When I first received Jesus as my savior, I met someone who was being severely tormented by the spirit of fear. When she left home and returned, she would literally go from room to room, checking under her bed, closets, and everywhere she could to make sure no one had come into her house while she was away. I hadn't seen anything like this before, and I could tell she did this often. The spirit of fear had rooted itself in her, and her actions revealed that the devil was tormenting her. This woman of God needed deliverance spiritually in order to see a natural result in her life. If she had gone to the doctor, the doctor might've told her she was paranoid and prescribed her medicine to calm her nerves. But the root of her problem was the spirit of fear. She needed to use the Word of God to destroy the spirit that had rooted itself in her.

Believers should never play with fear or treat it as something normal. The Word of God says, "For God hath not given us the spirit of fear; but of power, and of love, and of a sound mind," according to II Timothy 1:7 (KJV). We must speak the Word of God to fear. This is the only way it will flee from us.

Confession for Overcoming the Spirit of Fear

I stand in the authority that Jesus has given me, and I come against the spirit of fear that is operating in my life. The Lord rebuke you, you tormenting spirit *(Speak in the Holy Spirit and clap your hands)*. I decree and declare that Jesus has come that *I might have life and have it to the fullest* according to John 10:10, and I refuse to walk in torment because it is not God's will for me. I declare and decree you will not steal my peace. I bind you, and I loose your effects over me. Father, I declare according to the Word of God, *You have not given me the spirit of fear, but you have given me a spirit of power, love and a sound mind* (II Timothy 1:7), and I command *(Place both hands on your mind)* my mind to be sound right now in Jesus' name. I order you, spirit of fear, to leave me now, and I declare you have no power over me *(Speak in the Holy Spirit and clap your hands)*.

I command the peace of God that passes all understanding to rule my spirit, soul, and body in Jesus' name. I know without any doubt that my Father loves me and, because He loves me, I declare there is no fear in me. I order my mind to stop meditating on the problem, and my thoughts to be fixed on *what's true, just, pure, praiseworthy, lovely, and of a good report,* according to Philippians 4:8. I command my heart to be settled and receive the peace Jesus has given me. I declare as *I walk through the valley of the shadow of death, I will fear no evil because the LORD is with me* (Psalm 23:4). Father, your Word says *you are my refuge and strength and my ever present help in time of need*

(Psalm 46:1), and *the Lord is with me, so I will not be afraid. No one on earth can do anything to harm me* (Psalm 118:6). So, I believe I am free because according to I John 4:4, *Greater is He that is within me than He that is in the world.* I declare and decree that my heart, emotion, and mind are sound and fix on Jesus. The Word of God declares *whatsoever I bind on earth has already been bound in heaven, and whatsoever I loose on earth has already been loosed in heaven* (Matthew 18:18). Right now, I loose peace and joy over everything concerning me and my household, in the name of Jesus. Thank you, Father. I believe I am free, and *who the Son has set free is free indeed* (John 8:36) *(Speak in the Holy Spirit and clap your hands)* Amen!

Living in the Protection of God

The protection of God is for all believers who will take ownership of it. It is part of our kingdom benefit. Even though it is for every believer, the believer must make the transfer by faith to see it manifest in their lives. In the world, a rich man might have a great deal of money, but a lot of money is not most important. If he does not have good health, peace, and protection, he can't enjoy his wealth. In the kingdom of God, being wealthy and prosperous includes all aspects of life, such as mentally, physically, financially, and spiritually. God's protection is available to every believer, but he or she must take ownership of it to see it manifested in their lives. Just like all the other blessings God has given us, the believer must believe and walk in it by faith to see it manifest in their lives.

When we look at the life of Job, we see he was a wealthy man who had God's protection.

But, even though Job was prosperous, he walked in fear. Because he did, he opened the door to the enemy in his life. Fear gave Satan access to Job's life.

There is no way we can walk in God's protection and walk in fear at the same time. When we entertain the demonic spirit of fear, it gives Satan an entryway into our lives. The believer must resist fear and delight himself or herself in the love of God in order to walk in God's protection. This is the only way God's protection will become a reality in the life of a believer. Psalm 91:1 tells us that, when we dwell in the secret place of the Most High God, we will find protection under the feathers of His wings. In the secret place we are protected, and we commune with God. It's a place where Satan can't touch us because we are under God's protection.

Now, it's time to begin our confession for protection. We start by taking ownership of the promises of God. There's no need to ask for what has been already provided. Just claim it with your mouth!

Confession for Living in God's Protection

Thank you, Father. Your Word is life, *and it will never return void, but it will accomplish everything it is set out to do* (Isaiah 55:11). I decree and declare that I live in *the shelter of the Most High, and I am resting under the shadow of the Almighty God, and you, LORD, you alone are my refuge, a place of safety* (Psalm 91:1) *(Speak in the Holy Spirit and clap your hands)*. You are my God, and I put my trust in you. Thank you, Lord, for rescuing me from every trap, protecting me from deadly diseases, and covering me with the feathers of your wings. *Your faithful promises are my armor and my protection* (Psalm 91:4).

I will not be afraid of the terror by night, nor the dart that flies in the day. I will not be frightened of the diseases that stalk in the darkness, nor the disaster that strikes at midday because I know you are with me. Though I see thousands are falling on my right hand and on the left side, nothing by any means shall harm me. Only with my eyes I will see the wicked being punished. I declare and decree that *God, you are my refuge and my strength; you are my very present help in times when I'm in trouble* according to Psalm 91:5-9. *(Speak in the Holy Spirit and clap your hands)*. I confess right now that I'm taking refuge in you—the creator of heaven and earth. In you, I find shelter and no evil shall come near me. I declare that no plague will come near my home, job, school, business, church, children, or anything that concerns me. I order my ministering angels to take charge of me and anything pertaining to me and my household in the name of Jesus *(Speak in the Holy Spirit and clap your hands)*. I am confident my ministering angels are holding me up with their hands so *that I won't hurt my foot on a stone* (Psalm 91:12).

Today, I stand in my authority that Jesus Christ has given me, and I declare I *am trampling on lions and cobras and crushing fierce lions and serpents under my feet, and nothing by any means shall harm me* (Psalm 91:13). Father, I thank you for rescuing me from all of my troubles *and leading me beside the still waters* (Psalm 23:2). I receive your gift of *long life*, and I declare and decree *I will not die, but I will live to declare what the LORD has done* according to (Psalm 118:17), in Jesus' name. Amen!

Defending Healing in the Kingdom

Jehovah Rapha still heals! The Bible says, "How God anointed Jesus of Nazareth with the Holy Ghost and with power: who went about doing good, and healing all that were oppressed of the devil; for God was with Him" (Acts 10:38 KJV). We see here that sickness and diseases come from the devil; he is the one who is the oppressor of the people of God. But over two thousand years ago, according to Isaiah 53:5, *Jesus was wounded for our transgression; He was bruised for our iniquities: He was chastised for our peace, and with His stripes, we are healed.* Jesus paid the ultimate price, and healing has already been made available for anyone who will receive it.

Divine healing is not only for believers, but it is also for any human being who will accept this gift. In the Word of God, Jesus healed because of His compassionate love in response to faith, and through His Word. The Gentile woman who came to Jesus in Matthew 15 needing a miracle asked Jesus to deliver her daughter because she was demon-possessed. She used her faith and, because she did not give up, even when Jesus referred to her as a dog, her daughter was made whole.

The believer must understand because Jesus has paid it all on the cross, and because of His stripes, Jesus paid the price for our sickness—therefore, we are healed. It's essential for us not to pray from a position of begging or pleading with God, trying to get Him to heal us. Jesus has already paid the price for our healing. The Word of God says, "He sent His word, and healed them, and delivered them from their destructions" (Psalm 107:20 KJV).

Therefore, the Word of God is our spiritual medicine for healing of the body, and according to John 63:3, *it is spirit and life.* Healing can manifest in many different ways. First, healing will manifest when we take the Word and use it as medicine. We do this by meditating on it day and night until the *logos* Word becomes *rhema* or flesh. The Word of God tells us that believers can find good health through His Word. The Word must be kept in our eyes and hearts, and His Word will bring forth life (Proverbs 4:20-22).

Second, healing will manifest in the glory or in the presence of God, without any laying on of hands. When the atmosphere is ripe with the glory of God, healing will take place. Finally, healing becomes a reality when any believer with the gift and anointing of healing lays hands on the sick. The anointing destroys the yokes and sets the captives free (Isaiah 10:27). Believers filled with the power of the Holy Ghost lay their hands on the sick, and healing will manifest through the born-again believer.

Confessing my Healing in the Word

I decree and declare sickness and disease is not my portion because, over two thousand years ago, Jesus already paid the price for my healing, and I claim my healing as a blood-washed believer. I walk in divine health and, according to Exodus 23:25, Father, you said, *You will bless me with food and water, and you will protect me from illness.* So, right now, let this Word be established in my life. I call forth supernatural healing to manifest itself in my body in the mighty name of Jesus! I let go of all unforgiveness I am holding in my heart against any person now! I declare and decree my heart is free from hurt, bitterness, and resentment *(Speak in the Holy Spirit or clap your hands)*. I call on Jehovah Rapha, and I declare He has already forgiven me, *taken my sickness and diseases, and nailed them to the cross* (Isaiah 53:5). Father, your Word states that *many are the afflictions of the righteous, but you have already delivered me out of them all* (Psalm 34:19). I believe with all my heart I am made righteous because I am in Christ.

Hence, right now, Satan, the Lord rebukes you! I command every unclean spirit that has made its home in my body to leave me now. You have no place in my body because *my body is the temple of the Holy Spirit* (I Corinthians 6:19). I denounce you, and I command you spirit of oppression to leave me now *(Speak in the Holy Spirit and clap your hands)*. Healing already belongs to me because God's Word declares *that healing is His children's bread* (Matthew 15:26). I am a child of the Most High. Healing is my birthright. I command (fill in what the diagnosis is here) to leave me now. I believe the report of the LORD, and His report says, *I am healed*! I curse (fill in what the diagnosis is here) from your roots and command you to go back to your sender. The price has already been paid. I uproot every symptom from your root, and I release fire, fire over (fill in what the diagnosis is here), in the name of Jesus.

(Pray in the Holy Spirit or clap your hands.) Father, your Word says according to Exodus 15:26, *If I will listen carefully to the voice of the LORD my God and do what is right in your sight, obeying your commands and keeping all your decrees, then you will not make me suffer any of the diseases you sent on the Egyptians; for you are my LORD who heals me.* I speak to every blood vessel, tissue, cell, muscle, and organ in my body, and I command you to regulate, repair yourself, and line up with the Word of God. I take my healing now! I believe I walk in divine health, and I am prosperous in spirit, soul, and body! Thank you, Lord, for your supernatural wisdom concerning taking care of my health *(Speak in the Holy Spirit and clap your hands)*. Amen!

It's time for you to work your miracle!

Right there in your home, or wherever you are, check yourself and do what you couldn't do before. The pain is gone, and you are healed, in Jesus' name! Now, confess (Nahum 1:9). *This affliction shall not return a second time, in the name of Jesus! So, shall it be!*

Breaking Free from Ungodly Habits

A habit is a mental makeup or a normal manner of behavior. It is a behavior pattern acquired by frequent repetition, according to Merriam-Webster's Dictionary and Thesaurus. When we accept Jesus Christ as our personal Savior, the spirit is complete and lacking nothing, but the soul of a man must go through a process of renewing so it can be saved. Because a habit is a mental makeup, we know it's a stronghold. Satan tries to keep us walking in ungodly habits so he can try to trap us in our old mindset. Breaking the cycle cannot be done carnally, but it must be done through the washing of the Word.

Also, we must say, "No," to our old nature and decide to walk in our newfound freedom in Christ Jesus. Breaking loose from ungodly habits is critical for a believer, but we never have to do it alone because the Holy Spirit—the

Comforter—is always with us to help in a time of weakness. Also, believers must be willing to do whatever it takes to walk in freedom and to keep it. These confessions will only set the foundation for the believer. *Faith without works is dead*, according to James 2:17. Breaking free takes action, but as we make up our minds to spend time searching the Scriptures, studying, and meditating on the Word, we will begin to see change. Pay close attention to what you think because your thoughts become your actions, and they control your life. We must *cast down imaginations that are trying to exalt themselves against the knowledge of God* (II Corinthians 10:5) in order to live in freedom. Also, fasting and prayer is another spiritual tool we can use in order to break loose from ungodly habits and set us in motion for lasting change. *If you believe you are dealing with demonic or satanic attacks, seek additional spiritual help.*

Confession for Breaking Free from Ungodly Habits

Jehovah God, I believe I am redeemed from the curse of the law, and your Word declares *as you are, so am I in this world* (I John 4:17). With that knowledge, I take hold of my freedom now by faith from all ungodly habits. Mighty deliverer, I admit I desperately need you. Your Word declares that *you hear the cries of the righteous, and you will deliver me from all of my trouble* (Psalm 34:17) *(Pray in the Holy Spirit and clap your hands).* So, I come against and denounce (say your ungodly habit here) in my life that has hindered me from moving forward. I break your hold on me, my mind, my will, and my emotions in the name of Jesus!

Satan, I cut loose every spirit that has held my soul in prison. I command you to die, in the name of Jesus. I render your works powerless over me. I loose myself free from the habit of (say your ungodly habit here). I declare and decree you have no power over me because Jesus' blood has set me free. I bind every demonic spirit that has been using my members unto unrighteousness and sin. I commit myself to yield my members only unto righteousness according to Romans 6:13, and I loose your effect over me now *(Pray in the Holy Spirit and clap your hands).* I declare and decree that Jesus has already paid the price for my freedom, so I am set free from the habit of (say your ungodly habit here). The chain has been broken, and Satan, you have no foothold on me. I sprinkle the blood of Jesus over my mind, will, emotions, and body, and I believe I am free. I break forth by faith now out of every ungodly habit that has taken a hold of me. I thank you, Lord, right now that I am free and *who the son has set free is free indeed* (John 8:36). Amen!

Cultivating the Fruit of the Spirit

The Bible says, "But, the fruit of the Spirit is love, joy, peace, longsuffering, gentleness, goodness, faith, meekness, temperance: against such there is no law" (Galatians 5:22-23 KJV). Every born-again believer has the fruit of God's spirit on the inside of them because of the Holy Spirit who lives on the inside. So, every believer has the ability to bear fruit because he or she is connected to the true vine according to John 15:1-2 (KJV). The Word of God says, "I am the true vine, and My Father is the husbandman. Every branch in me that beareth not fruit he takes away, and every branch that beareth fruit, he pruneth, that it may bring more fruit." Since we are joined to the true vine, we bear much fruit. According to *Vine's Complete Expository Dictionary*, a fruit is the visible expression of power, working inwardly and invisibly; it is the character of the fruit, being evidence of the character of power producing it.

These fruits are the characters of God, and they must be cultivated in order to see them manifested on the outside of the believer. It is during a season of testing, trials, and challenges that the fruit of God's spirit is cultivated. When we allow ourselves to go through the process of testing, our fruit will grow. For example, the fruit of longsuffering is cultivated only when the believer goes through a season of waiting because, when we remain steadfast during a time of waiting, our endurance will be developed, and the faith of the believer will move to another level. Also, when we bear much fruit, we become a great testimony to win souls for the kingdom of God. Please understand, declaring this confession will not make the fruit show up automatically in your life. However, when you begin to confess this confession, it will allow you to be conscious of the fact you must be patient with yourself and endure the process, so God's Word can produce in your life. As you go through your day, I encourage you to begin taking note of which fruit of the spirit is exhibited in your life and which ones are not. Then, pray, read your Word, and ask God for the strength to go through the process while the fruit is being developed.

Confession for Cultivating the Fruit of the Spirit

Thank you, Jehovah Shalom, for you are my *peace that surpasses all understanding* (Philippians 4:7). So, now, according to Galatians 5:22-23, I declare I no longer walk in the flesh, but in the fruit of God's spirit that is in me, which is love, joy, peace, longsuffering, gentleness, goodness, faith, meekness, and temperance. I believe and confess *that greater is He that is in me than he that is in the world* (I John 4:4). Because He lives in me, I no longer live after my flesh, but after the Spirit. Father, your Word declares if I *ask, it shall be given; if I seek, I will find; and if I knock, the door will be opened to me* (Matthew 7:7). So, I ask you, Father, to fill me afresh with your Holy Spirit because I am one with you *(Pray in the Holy Spirit and clap your hands).*

I declare and decree by faith the fruit of your spirit is already reigning through my life and according to Isaiah 40:31, *those who wait on you shall have renewed strength.* So I thank you that my strength is renewed *(Pray in the Holy Spirit and clap your hands).* I give you praise and thanks in every situation I find myself in because the *testing of my faith is producing patience* according to James 1:3. I ask right now, Father, for a fresh encounter with your unconditional love and compassion. Help me Father, to *rejoice in hope; patient in tribulation, and continuing in prayer* according to Roman 12:12. Break my heart, Lord, for what breaks your heart.

As I seek after cultivating the fruit of your spirit in my life, I believe and receive by faith the fruit of (fill in here the fruit you need developed in your life) is manifesting itself through me now, in Jesus' name. Father, I have received your grace, and I realize *no good thing will you withhold from me because I walk upright before you* (Psalm 84:11). I believe I will see the fruit of (fill in the fruit here) manifesting in my life in abundance, in the name of Jesus. Amen!

Living With Divine Purpose and Destiny

How do you feel when the alarm clock goes off on a Monday morning? Are you happy or are you sad? Can you name at least three things you like about your job, excluding the money? Do you feel empty, or do you feel like something is missing in your life? Do you find your job boring or uninteresting? Are you working at your job only because it's paying your bills? What about your home life? Do you get lonely at times? Even when your spouse is there? Well, if you answered, "Yes" to these questions, this could be an indication you have not yet discovered your God-given purpose.

The unhappiness or emptiness you may be feeling could be because your purpose is still locked up on the inside of you, and you have not yet discovered it. Every human being was born with a motivational gift according to Romans 12:6-8. These are the gifts God placed on the inside of every human being to use for the benefit of others and for the glory of God. Maybe you dreamt of doing something great, but you haven't sought after it because you have been so caught up paying bills. Perhaps the spirit of fear has kept you bound for a very long time. I believe our true destiny is tied to our purpose in God.

Before we were in our mother's womb, God placed purpose and destiny on the inside of each of us, and we must not die with the purpose and destiny God placed inside of us. Believers must fulfill their God-given assignment on this earth so we can bring glory to God. Myles Munroe once said, "The cemetery is the richest place on earth because many people die with purpose on the inside of them." While they were living, they did not discover their purpose, or maybe, they were too afraid to go after their dreams. So, as a result, many died without completing their divine mission on earth. Don't let this be you! Get in the position of communing with God so you can discover your God-given purpose. Don't be afraid to step out in faith. Your wealth is tied up in your purpose! Don't die full; die empty!

Confession for Living With Divine Purpose and Destiny

Father, in the mighty name of Jesus, I am blessed of the Lord, and your Word declares *before you formed me in my mother's belly, you knew me* (Jeremiah 1:5), and *you know the plans you have for me—they are plans of good and not of evil, to take me to my expected end* (Jeremiah 29:11). So, I bind every spirit of stagnation that is trying to hinder my purpose and my destiny from going forth. Satan, the Lord rebukes you! *(Pray in the Holy Spirit and clap your hands).* I break your hold, and I command you spirit of Pharaoh to loose me and let me go. I render your works *powerless*! *(Pray in the Holy Spirit and clap your hands).* I declare right now the blood of Jesus covers my purpose and destiny, and I will not die without completing my divine purpose!

(Place your hands on your stomach) say, I call forth my purpose, and I command you to *come forth now* in Jesus' name! I declare *my gifts are making room for me and bringing me before great men* according to Proverbs 18:16. I command doors of opportunity to fly open now! I bind every spirit of limbo. I curse you! *(Pray in the Holy Spirit or clap your hands).* I call forth, a business idea, ministry, job, and every unborn purpose, and I command the heavens to be opened and the favor of God to fall on me now, in Jesus' name. I command the wind of God to blow in my direction with abundance of rain and favor to fall on me now *(Pray in the Holy Spirit or clap your hands)*. I declare I will die empty, and I will not die prematurely or before my time! God's purpose is prevailing in me, and everything I put my hands to do is already blessed *(Pray in the Holy Spirit or clap your hands)*. Father, you have begun a good work in me, and I believe *you are faithful to complete it to the very end* according to Philippians 1:6. I decree I am increasing in wisdom, statue, and favor with God and with men according to Luke 2:52, in Jesus' name. Amen!

The Confession of a Tither

I have met so many believers who believe in the Word of God, but believe it's not the will of God for them to return a tithe to the Lord. They believe tithing is only for the people in the Old Testament, and we are not required to tithe under grace because the new covenant does not require us to give a tithe. But this is not true at all!

According to *Vine's Complete Expository Dictionary*, the word *tithe* is a Hebrew word *dekatoo*, which means tenth. The tenth belongs to God; He has set it apart for Himself; it's holy. The Bible says Abram tithed to Melchizedek, the High Priest (Genesis 14:20); Melchizedek symbolizes a type of Jesus in the Old Testament according to Genesis 14:20. But, Jesus is the High Priest forever after the order of Melchizedek (Hebrews 7:17).

Therefore, today, when we return our tithes to our local church, we are returning through Abraham to Jesus, who is the great High Priest. The first portion of our earnings belongs to the great High Priest, and He promises, in return, to rebuke Satan for our sakes and bless us in return. The Word of God declares in Malachi 3:10 (KJV), "Bring ye all the tithes into the storehouse, that there may be meat in mine house and prove me now herewith, saith the LORD of hosts, if I will not open you the windows of heaven, and pour you out a blessing, that there shall not be room enough to receive it." Tithing is done out of a heart of love and obedience to God, not man.

I believe the tithe also connects believers with the blessings of God. Every believer is commanded to return a tenth of their earnings to God. The tithe is not a payment to God, but we are obeying His Word because we love Him. It takes faith, trust, and obedience in God's Word to tithe. Hearing the Word preached on the tithe is essential. The tithe has many benefits. Again, God Himself promises that *He will rebuke the devourer for our sake, and our fruit will not fall off the tree before its time* (Malachi 3:11). When the believer returns the tithe to the Lord, the believer's crops receive protection. After we do our part, the Lord of the harvest will do His part. Therefore, when Satan tries to interfere with the fruit (what belongs to us) of our ground, we can boldly respond to Satan by saying, "Satan, the Lord rebukes you. I am a tither."

The tithe is not optional. Please understand, God is not going to pressure anyone to tithe. He won't love us less because we don't tithe. But, if the believer wants to see the blessing of the Lord in their finances, he or she must tithe.

If the believer doesn't tithe, Satan has access to the believer's possessions. Here is an example of what I mean. I encountered a woman of God, via an international prayer line, who was having a hard time keeping Satan away from her belongings. The woman of God asked me for prayer after she told me three times in a row someone broke into her apartment and stole from her. While I was praying, the Holy Spirit spoke to me and said, "She doesn't need prayers; she needs to become a tither." So, I stepped out on faith and asked the woman if she was a tither. Immediately, she said, "No, I am not a tither." I knew I had heard the voice of God, but I felt a bit uncomfortable asking this woman if she was a tither. That very day, I learned sometimes the turbulence in the life of some believers is an indication they are not tithing. The Holy Spirit allowed me to encourage her to become a tither, and I prayed that she would obey God.

The Confession of a Tither

Father, I come to you in the name of a tither. I believe I remained faithful to do what you have commanded me to do, so I thank you that *Satan has been rebuked for my sake, and I declare the window of heaven is opened to me now, and the fruit of my ground will never be destroyed* according to Malachi 3:10-11 *(Pray in the Holy Spirit or clap your hands)!* Hence, lack is not my portion, and I confess because I am in covenant with you; opportunities, open doors, and favor are looking for me! I speak favor over my business, ministry, children, house, and everything that concerns me. According to Mark 11:23, I decree and declare, *every mountain in my life, I command you to move* in Jesus' name. I speak to my mountain of (fill in an obstacle here) to be cast into the sea and be gone now. I am a tither, and I command every mountain of financial bondage to fall in the mighty name of Jesus. I have no doubt in my mind that my financial chains of lack have been broken because I am the righteousness of God. I believe because I have obeyed God's Word and returned my tithe into the storehouse, doors of opportunities are mine today. Thank you, Lord, because I am a tither, I will not suffer storage, layoff, and misfortune because you have rebuked the hands of the destroyer *(Pray in the Holy Spirit or clap your hands).* You have opened doors and windows of blessing in my life, and because I am a seed of Abraham, every promise you made with him, according to Genesis 12:1-3, belongs to me. I have obeyed your Word and returned my tithe to the great High Priest, and I believe the windows of heaven are open to me now, and the blessings of the Lord are overtaking me. I call forth increase, favor, open doors, the goodness of God, divine surprises, promotion and expansion in business, and on everything I put my hands to do. I decree and declare that everything my hands touch will prosper according to Deuteronomy 30:9 because I am a tither. Amen!

Walking in Debt Freedom

The kingdom of God has its own financial system. But, Satan is the god of this world's Babylonian system. Debt is not the will of God for the believer. In fact, debt is part of the curse according to Deuteronomy 28:44. The Word of God declares we *shall have no need to borrow, and the borrower is a servant to the lender* (Proverbs 22:7). A servant is a person who performs duties for another person. Because we are in debt, we are servants to the person we owe. As a matter of fact, the only thing a blood-washed believer should owe to a man is love according to Romans 13:8. But, the world's system functions on debt—buy now and pay later. America and many other countries worldwide are in billions or even trillions of dollars in debt. Debt is a financial sickness. If we were to take a poll to see how many born-again believers are in debt, the outcome would be frightening. Most believers are in debt, and most have no desire to live debt free.

IF YOU CHANGE YOUR WORDS, YOU'LL CHANGE YOUR LIFE!

Have you ever noticed when you try to buy something from the nearest department store, you will find there are no incentives for consumers who are paying cash? All the incentives are geared toward consumers who will open a credit account. If you walk in any department or grocery store, the cashier will ask, "What credit card will you be using?" The reason for this is this world functions on credit.

Being in debt is serious business! It will pass down from generation to generation, if someone in the family doesn't get a breakthrough in their finances in their lifetime. Also, in our society today, most college students spend four years in college. Afterward, they can't even enjoy the fruits of their labor right away because, when they graduate, they are drowning in thousands of dollars of debt. This is not the will of God for them. God's desire is for believers to walk in debt freedom and live that way. Seeking God and renewing our minds according to the Word is essential in order to live debt free.

Let's start confessing the Word over our debt and make a decision to do what the Holy Spirit tells us to do concerning getting out of debt. Colossians 2:14 reminds us that Jesus *canceled the record of the charges against us and took them away by nailing them to the cross.* Jesus not only took away our sins on the cross, but He also set us free from debt. When He said it was finished—our physical, mental, spiritual, and financial realities were all included with Him on the cross. Therefore, the believer stands in faith in order to see the manifestation of what Jesus has already made possible for us.

Confession for Walking in Debt Freedom

Father, I confess I have sinned against you. I admit I have walked contrary to your Word concerning my financial affairs, and I ask you to forgive me. Your Word declares according to Romans 13:8, *to owe no man anything but love*, and I believe just like you have nailed all my sins to the cross, you have nailed all my financial debt to the cross *(Pray in the Holy Spirit or clap your hands)*. Forgive me, Father, for mishandling my financial affairs and yoking myself with unbelievers. From this day forward, I choose your will, and I declare and decree that I operate financially according to your Word. Your Word says, *You are my shepherd, and I have all that I need* according to Psalm 23:1 (NLT) *(Pray in the Holy Spirit or clap your hands)*.

Father, I ask you now for a debt cancellation plan, and that you would give me the courage to do what you say. I bind the spirit of debt that is in operation in my life, and I curse you from your roots *(Pray in the Holy Spirit or clap your hands)*. I loose the forces of heaven into my financial affairs right now. I have sown my seeds for supernatural debt cancellation and to break the spirit of debt off my life, and I dispatch harvesting angels of God to go out and bring in my harvest from the east, west, north, and south. I command *money* cometh to me now, in the name of Jesus! I decree the "wealth of the wicked" is mine, and wealth and riches are in my house (Psalm 112:3). I decree and declare I operate financially according to kingdom principles. I claim this is my due season because I have sown my seed for debt freedom, and I command a hundredfold return to come to me now, in the name of Jesus.

Father, you can trust me to live debt free, and you can do business through me. I declare nations are looking at me and calling me blessed. I declare I am the head, and I am not the tail. *I am the lender and not the borrower* (Deuteronomy 28:13). I believe the yokes of debt, lack, poverty, and insufficiency have been broken off my life, and I will never again be broke or in bondage to a lender another day in my life, in Jesus' name *(Pray in the Spirit or clap your hands)*. Amen!

Walking in Kingdom Prosperity

As I stated in the previous confession, to make a transfer to financial breakthrough from the spiritual world to the natural world, there must be a decision to get out of debt and to stay out. But, above all, "But first and most importantly seek (aim at, strive after) His kingdom and His righteousness [His way of doing and being right- the attitude and character of God], and all these things will be given to you, also" (Matthew 6:33 AMP). When we seek God first, and His right way of living above anything else, God will bless us in return, and we will experience kingdom prosperity.

Most believers would like to live in prosperity, but they are not willing to do what it takes to make the transfer. Kingdom prosperity is a benefit for every born-again believer. There is no way God would prosper some believers and not prosper others. If this were true, then God would be a respecter of persons.

A prosperous believer begins on the inside of the man, then flows to the outside. When the inside of the man becomes "fat" with the Word of God, then the man will become prosperous in the world he lives in (III John 1:2). Even though the man's prosperity comes from getting *fat* on the Word of God, what he believes must be demonstrated through a response to God's Word.

The Word of God declares *as long as the earth remains, there will be seedtime and harvest* (Genesis 8:22). The only way in the kingdom of God to be prosperous, financially, is through receiving our spiritual inheritance, walking in obedience toward God, and through our giving. God has established four types of giving so that believers can make the wealth transfer from the spiritual world to the natural world.

First, we spoke about the tithe, earlier, which is a tenth or the first portion—the sacred part of our income. Second, the firstfruit is an act of honor, which goes to either the pastor or the church of God (Proverbs 3:9). An example of the firstfruit is if someone starts a new job, their first check is the firstfruit. Or if they get a raise of ten dollars on their job, then the ten dollars is their firstfruit, given once. Thirdly, alms are another type of giving, which is giving to the poor, with a compassionate heart. The Bible says angels were released because of Cornelius, the Gentile, who prayed and gave alms to the poor in Acts 10:3-4. Alms giving is to the poor, so it must be done in secret. But, in return, God will repay the believer for his or her giving to the poor (Matthew 6:1-4). Whatever amount the believer gives to the poor, he or she is lending it to God.

Finally, when a seed is planted in fertile soil, the return will be thirty, sixty, or a hundred-fold according to Matthew 13:8. This seed will produce the most significant gain for the believer. According to II Corinthians 9:7, *the Lord loves a cheerful giver*. So having the right attitude while giving is important.

The believer becomes prosperous in the kingdom for several reasons. One reason is to fulfill the covenant God made with Abraham, our father of faith. The promise God made with Abraham and his descendants included: *God would bless him and make him a blessing; He would curse or bless those who cursed or blessed him. He would make his name great, and all the families of the earth would be blessed through him* (Genesis 12:1-3). Therefore, the Bible says, *because we are in Christ, then we are Abraham's seed and heirs according to the promise* (Galatians

3:29). Consequently, God blesses us so this promise He made with Abraham will become a reality in us today (Deuteronomy 8:18). Likewise, we are blessed, so we can be a blessing. God will use us to build up His kingdom, and we can enjoy life and live a life of abundance according to (John 10:10).

Confession for Kingdom Prosperity

El Shaddai, I call on you because you are the All-Sufficient One! In you, there is no lack. You are the God of abundance. *Lord, be magnified, which has pleasure in the prosperity of* (Fill your name in here) (Psalm 35:27). *Your blessings make me rich and add no sorrow* according to Proverbs 10:22. I decree the hundred-fold return is working for me, and I declare and decree I am prosperous in every area of my life. My eyes are open to creative ways to increase financially *(Speak in the Holy Spirit or clap your hands)*. I am a money magnet. Lack is not my portion. Everywhere I go, money finds me. I have several avenues of wealth coming through my hands, and I call everything I touch to be blessed. *Though He was rich, yet for my sake He became poor, so that I through His poverty am made rich* (II Corinthians 8:9). This is why *wealth and riches are in my house, and my righteousness endures forever* according to Psalm 112:3. I declare the wealth of the sinner is no longer laid up for me, but it is transferred to me (Proverbs 13:22), and I have already entered into my wealthy place *(Speak in the Holy Spirit or clap your hands).*

I believe by faith my heart is pure, so the Lord can channel kingdom wealth through me. I decree and declare I am a kingdom distributor of wealth; money in abundance is looking for me. I call forth *money*, "Come to me now from the four corners of this world, in the name of Jesus!" I command you, money, to supernaturally transfer into my bank account, come in my mailbox, and come anyway God sees fit, in the name of Jesus. My very nature attracts money, and the fear of lack is broken off of me. I have sowed my seed for supernatural abundance, and I live in daily expectation of abundance. Daily, *I am loaded with benefits* (Psalm 68:19). I call forth *harvest* to come to me now. I have sowed bountifully, and I call forth a bountiful harvest to come to me now. I declare the fruit of my hands are blessed. *I am walking in the favor of God and with men, and my gifts are making room for me and bringing me before great men* according to Proverbs 18:16. I commit myself to establishing the kingdom of God on the earth, to bring aid to the poor, to give to the work of the Lord, and to be the hands and feet of Jesus! I speak to the winds of God, and I command them to blow money, favor, and open doors in my direction *(Speak in the Holy Spirit or clap your hands)*. I release my ministering angels of God to go out and bring me back my harvest from the four corners of the earth *(Speak in the Holy Spirit or clap your hands)*. I decree and declare I will *never* be broke another day in my life, in Jesus' name. Thank you, Lord, it is done! So, let it be!

Believing God for Employment

There was a time in my life, prior to writing this book, when I worked with children. Although I enjoyed working with children, I always felt as though there was something missing in my life, and God was calling me to do something different. I worked for the government making pretty decent money—more than I ever made working with children. But I still felt as though there was a void.

During this time of considering where to go with my career, my prayer life increased tremendously. One day as I walked through my front door from work, I lifted my head and hands up before the Lord and said out loud, "God, I feel like something is missing. There has got to be more to life than this!" Then, I heard the voice of the Holy Spirit say, "I want you to stay home full-time and write." I asked, "Write what?" I thought to myself it must be the voice of the devil because we had just brought a new home? My husband would probably think I was hearing things.

But, I knew if it was God, He had a better plan for my life. So I prayed and took a step of faith. Today, I am so glad I obeyed God because my life has completely taken off in a direction for the better. I just finished Bible College, obtaining my Bachelor of Arts in Religious Studies, and I no longer feel that void. God is using me significantly.

I wanted to start this section sharing my testimony because I want to make sure you know, without a doubt, that you know for sure what you have been called to do. This is important because you may end up one year from now in the same place where you are today. I shared my testimony with you because I believe some of you who are reading this should stop and examine yourself and ask yourself, "Is what I'm pursuing something God ordained, or is it something I am doing just to make money?" Many believers spend years of their life outside of the will of God, chasing a dream that is not from God.

Let us look at the original way man survived in the garden. Adam was created to create a living and not to earn one. In fact, after the fall, part of the curse is that man had to sweat (Hebrew toil) for a living because his sin had consequences. Today, believers are redeemed from the curse of Adam because Jesus was cursed in our place according to Galatians 3:13, and He restored us back to God's original intent for mankind. This is why there should be no sweating or toiling, trying to earn a living. We must operate in man's original state; we must seek God for creative ways to create increase. Believers must know who they are in God, discover their purpose, and go after it with every fiber of their being.

I believe that before you start praying to find employment, you should make sure it's God's plan for your life. I am not saying everyone in the kingdom is called to have a business or to be in ministry full-time. But, make sure whatever it is, is God's will.

The Apostle Paul wrote to the Corinthian church *if a man does not work, he doesn't eat* (II Thessalonians 3:10). However, wherever you find purpose, divine prosperity is waiting for you.

Confession for Believing God for Employment

Father, your Word is true, and right now, I seek your wisdom concerning my employment. I thank you in advance for directing my path and leading me to find your will for my life. I believe I was created for such a time as this (Esther 4:14), and I walk in my dominion as I lay hold of your promises for my life. I thank you right now because I am your child, and you love me. I know you have already opened unto me doors of opportunity and favor. My eyes and ears are open to your voice. So, I am standing on your Word, believing and decreeing that everything *I need has already been provided before the foundation of the world* according to (II Peter 1:3).

I am willing to work with my hands, so I will lack nothing. I come against the spirit of fear and doubt that has been assigned to my life to stop me from moving forward *(Speak in the Holy Spirit or clap your hands)*. I speak to *every principality, power, ruler of darkness, and every spiritual wickedness in heavenly places* that has been trying to frustrate my dreams from coming to pass *(Speak in the Holy Spirit or clap your hands)*. I declare and decree that God, you are Jehovah Jireh, and I shall not want for anything (Psalm 23:1). Thank you, Father, that all *your grace, every favor, and earthly blessing comes to me in abundance, so I may always, and under all circumstances, and whatever my need may be, be self-sufficient—possessing enough to require no aid or support and furnished in abundance for every good work and charitable donation* according to II Corinthians 9:8 (AMPC) *(Speak in the Holy Spirit or clap your hands)*.

I am free from worry, doubt, anxiety, and frustration. I command my mind to settle down and receive the *shalom* Jesus has given me. I enter into your rest as I seek your will. In all things and in every circumstance, I give you thanks. I say, Thank you, Father, because I know all of my needs have already been met according to your riches in glory by Christ Jesus our Lord (Philippians 4:19). Father, I thank you in advance for supplying a job, opening doors for ministry, college tuition paid, or for the releasing of a business idea that will change my life in Jesus' name. Amen!

Living with Good Health

If a believer is victorious in every area of their life but does not have good health, then it is not correct to say he or she walks in kingdom prosperity. In the kingdom, prosperity should manifest in every area of our lives. The Bible says in III John 2 (KJV), "Beloved, I wish above all things that thou mayest prosper and be in health, even as thy soul prospereth." This verse tells us our physical health is just as important as our spiritual health. It is the will of God for every believer to manifest good health, which is a benefit of the kingdom. The Word of God declares faith without works (Greek word, *ergon,* which means good deeds or an action) is dead according to James 2:17. We take ownership of having good health by faith in order to see manifestation of it. This is done by having good nutrition, adequate sleep, exercising regularly, and drinking plenty of water.

We can be anointed and have a great business, ministry, or be an important leader, but if we don't maintain good nutrition, we will have a hard time being who God calls us to be because of poor health. As mentioned before, *our bodies are the temple of the Holy Spirit* according to I Corinthians 6:19, and we must be a good steward of it. The Holy Spirit, who is the Comforter, will reveal to us what we should do in order to walk in good health.

I heard a profound testimony from a great man of God. He was experiencing pain in his body. But instead of going directly to the doctor, he decided to go away for a period and seek God concerning his matter. God revealed to him he had been drinking too much coffee and needed to stop. When he stopped drinking coffee, the pain left him. Please understand, I am not advocating against seeing your doctor. What I am saying is that God is our source of life, and when we consult Him concerning our physical body, He will reveal to us what we need to know.

Confession for Good Health

Father, I commit myself to take hold of your Word by faith and walk in and pursue good health. I recognize my body is *the temple of the Holy Spirit* according to I Corinthians 6:19, and I am adding to my faith to do whatever needs to be done in order to walk in good health. I commit myself to eat the right foods and make it my duty to exercise. I declare and decree my sleep is sweet. Forgive me, Father, for not being a good steward over my body thus far. I choose right now to turn away and walk in your will concerning good health. I believe you are *satisfying me with long life* (Psalm 91:16), and *I am prosperous and in good health, even while my soul is prospering* (III John 2). Father, I realize I have been "bought with a price," and I glorify you in my body. So help me to follow your leading concerning my body. I confess right now that I have abundant life and neither sickness nor disease is my portion, in Jesus' name. I bind the spirit of greed that has taken root in me *(Speak in the Holy Spirit or clap your hands)*. I command you, spirit of gluttony, to leave me now! I denounce you, and I declare you have no power over me *(Speak in the Holy Spirit or clap your hands)*.

I loose healthy habits over me, and I am free from the bondage of my past. I cover all the gates to my heart with the blood of Jesus. I cover my eyes, ears, mouth, and nose with the blood of Jesus. I thank you, Comforter, for helping me to renew my mind concerning my eating habits. I reject all that this world has to offer me. I loose myself from the *lust of the flesh, the lust of the eyes, and the pride of life* according to I John 2:15-17. I break away right now from sugars, fatty foods, and high starches. I believe and receive the instruction from you, Father, for my weight loss or weight maintenance, and thank you, Lord, in advance for supernatural strength to make this a lifestyle. Thank you for restoring my health, in Jesus' name. Amen!

Standing in Faith for an Unsaved Loved One

When we are standing in faith for the salvation of our unsaved loved ones, the believer must realize it's God's desire *that all men be saved and come to the knowledge of Him* (I Timothy 2:4). It's difficult to witness our loved ones fall into various traps of the enemy by walking in sin. In my personal life, I have seen family members live in sin, and my heart aches because, I know if they turn their hearts to God, they will be better off. But the Holy Spirit always reminds me of the season when I was living in sin. It was God's grace and mercy that brought me into the light. Therefore, I commit myself to pray fervently for those family members to receive the free gifts of grace and mercy in their lives.

When we are standing in the gap for the salvation of our unsaved loved ones, we must understand the underlying issue is Satan. *He is the one who has blinded their minds, preventing them from receiving the gospel of Jesus,* according to II Corinthians 4:4. He is using their members to do unrighteous acts. Satan and his demonic counterparts are spirits, and they need a vessel to use because they are useless without it.

But, the Bible says, "I tell you, you can pray for anything, and if you believe that you've received it, it will be yours," (Mark 11:24 NLT). Therefore, it is critical that our words line up to what we are praying. Too often, believers pray about their unsaved loved ones and, right after they have prayed, begin with their own words, canceling out their prayers. *Life and death are in the power of our tongue* according to Proverbs 18:21. So, Satan is waiting for our words in order to open the portal of hell in our world; so, we must choose to speak life, not death. Pray that God will *send a laborer to deliver* (Matthew 9:38) the good news of the gospel, *or to plant or water the seed that has already been sown* (I Corinthians 3:6) in your unsaved loved ones. Remember, never stop praying while you rest and wait patiently in expectation for their salvation.

Confession for Unsaved Loved Ones

Jehovah Tsidkenu, you are our righteousness, and I stand in the gap for the salvation of (fill in the blank with name(s) here). Your Word declares *it is your will that none will perish, but for all to come unto the knowledge of the truth* (I Timothy 2:4), and, LORD, *you are not slack concerning your promises* according to II Peter 3:9. So, today, I thank you in advance for the salvation of (fill in the blank with name(s) here). I speak to every demonic and satanic spirit in operation. I bind you now, and I command you to loose your effects in the lives of (fill in the blank with name(s) here) *(Pray in the Holy Spirit or clap your hands)*.

I am the righteousness of God, and I am a carrier of the authority of Jesus. So, I command the veil that has been blinding the eyes, heart, and mind of (fill in the blank with name(s) here) to be removed now! I declare and decree (fill in the blank with name(s) here) *spiritual eyes of understanding to be enlightened; that* he/she/they *may know what is the hope of* (fill in the blank with name(s) here) *calling and what is the riches of the glory of his inheritance* according to Ephesians 1:18 *(Pray in the Holy Spirit or clap your hands)*.

IF YOU CHANGE YOUR WORDS, YOU'LL CHANGE YOUR LIFE!

I decree and declare by faith that (fill in the blank with name(s) here) are the righteousness of God, and he/she/they obey godly instructions. I release laborers across their path that are equipped with the gospel of salvation to minister to them. I command every chain in their lives to fall right now *(Pray in the Holy Spirit or clap your hands)*. Fall, now! I break every power of darkness, every plan and plot in the lives of (fill in the blank with name(s) here). I believe the power of the Holy Spirit is activated in their lives, *and no weapon that has been formed against them will prosper* according to Isaiah 54:17.

Thank you, Father, that (fill in the blank with name(s) here) have been recovered from the snare of the enemy and are saved, sanctified, spirit-filled, well on their way to renewing their minds, and discovering who they are in Christ Jesus. Thank you, Father, for watching over your Word, and I believe (fill in the blank with name(s) here) are free because *He who the son has set free, is free indeed,* in Jesus' name (John 8:36). Amen!

Begin to thank God in advance for the salvation of your loved ones!

Defeating Unbelief, Doubt, and Frustration

The spirit of unbelief is serious business. The enemy uses it as a weapon to hinder believers from receiving the blessings of God. In Mark 6:5, the Bible says Jesus couldn't perform any miracles in His hometown because of the people's unbelief. The people in Jesus' home-town did not experience Jesus in His fullness because they did not believe. But, the Bible tells us clearly *that the just shall live by (faith)*, believing, not doubting, according to Romans 1:17. What is it we must believe? We must believe in the finished work of the cross.

When a believer finds himself or herself walking in unbelief, he or she can't expect to receive anything from God. As a matter of fact, Jesus rebuked His disciples several times in the Word of God because of their unbelief.

Unbelief is a spirit, and it operates with doubt, fear, and frustration. The enemy uses unbelief by planting a seed in our mind, so that what we say will become contrary to the Word of God. When unbelief comes our way, we are focusing on our situation instead of the problem-solver, Jesus. Therefore, we can't tolerate unbelief; once it shows up, the believer must use the sword of the spirit to demolish it. Also, in Mark 9:28, when the disciples asked Jesus why they couldn't cast a demon out of a boy, Jesus replied, "This kind can be cast out only by prayer and fasting," (Mark 9:29 NLT). So, clearly, we see the cure for unbelief is fasting and praying. Now, it's time to destroy the spirit of unbelief, doubt, fear, and frustration by using the Word of God. But, if unbelief persists in your life, then prayer and fasting will help you break free.

Confession for Defeating the Spirit of Unbelief, Doubt, and Frustration

In Jesus' name, I speak to the spirit of unbelief, doubt, and frustration. I denounce you; you have no place in me. I choose to take hold of the promises of God, and I'm waiting patiently for the Lord to show up in my life *(Pray in the Holy Spirit or clap your hands)*. I stand in my authority Jesus has given me, and I speak to the mountain of unbelief, doubt, fear, and frustration, and I command you to move according to Mark 11:24 *(Pray in the Holy Spirit or clap your hands)*. Jesus is Lord in my life, and I believe His report over every situation in my life. I refuse to be troubled by my situation. *Greater is He that is in me than he that is in the world* according to I John 4:4, and because the greater one lives in me, the spirits of unbelief, doubt, and frustration are trespassing in me, so I command unbelief to bow your knees at the name of *Jesus (Pray in the Holy Spirit or clap your hands)*.

As I stand on every promise you have given me concerning (fill in whatever your situation is here), I decree manifestation is already mine. I confess that I am walking by faith and not by sight (II Corinthians 5:7), and I am not moved by what I feel, hear, or what it looks like. I am only moved by the Word of God, and I am free from unbelief, doubt, and frustration. No weapon that is formed against me or anything pertaining to me will prosper. Every tongue that has risen up against me in judgment, I command it to be condemned, in the name of Jesus (Isaiah 54:17). I confess Jesus is Lord over my mind, and I declare I have the mind of Christ according to I Corinthians 2:16, and I declare my mind is in perfect peace. I confess this is my day of my breakthrough, deliverance, and visitation from the Lord. Thank you, Father, that your Son has set me free. Therefore, I believe I am free in the mighty name of Jesus (John 8:38). So, let it be!

Breaking Through to a Successful Business

I always thought great success would fall into our laps because we made Jesus the Lord of our lives. I would say at times, since I'm already blessed, I don't have to do anything but to live, and a successful life will eventually show up in my life. Please understand me clearly: I am not saying success must be earned because nothing God has given us can be earned. But, it's by God's grace and mercy that He has already blessed us. Everything He has given us, as believers, we are not qualified to have it, nor do we deserve it. It is because of the love of God that we have anything. Great and lasting success comes from the Lord. It is a benefit that is available to every born-again believer (spiritually), but believers must fight the fight of faith to obtain it and enable the transfer from the spiritual world to the natural world by faith. When we seek God and His kingdom, the believer becomes spiritually healthy. Before long, what is on the inside of him or her will manifest on the outside.

The believer's success does not depend on God; it is our responsibility to make the transfer. In Joshua 1:8 (KJV), it tells us, "This book of the law shall not depart out of (fill in your name here) mouth; but (fill in your name here) shalt meditate therein day and night, that (fill in your name here) mayest observe to do according to all that is written therein. Then (fill in your name here) shalt make thy way prosperous, and then (fill in your name here), thou shalt have good success." So, now, let me ask you a question. "Who is the one responsible for your success?" You and I are accountable for our own success; God is not! God has already equipped us with everything we need to become successful. Moreover, a successful business that is built on the Word of God is already designed to become prosperous. God has already given believers the power to get wealth according to Deuteronomy 8:18, but we have a part to play in making it a reality in our lives. The believer must be *willing and obedient. Only then, shall we eat the good of the land* (Isaiah 1:19).

Confession for Kingdom Success in Business and Ministry

I believe and receive by faith that *everything I ever need for my life and godly living has already been given to me* according to II Peter 1:3, and today, I am choosing to take what has been given to me by faith. I am highly favored by God, and *crowned with glory and honor* according to (Psalm 8:5), and I believe *the fruit of my hands is already blessed* according to Psalm 128:2. I am successful, rich, and have a prosperous life, and *my gifts have already made room for me and are bringing me before kings, nations, and great men* (Proverbs 18:16). I decree and declare doors of favor and opportunity are looking for me now, and *the blessing of the Lord is making me rich and adds no sorrow* (Proverbs 10:22) *(Pray in the Holy Spirit or clap your hands).*

I declare by faith I am the tree that is planted by the river bank, and this is my season to bring forth abundant fruit. Whatever I put my hands to do is prospering according to Psalm 1:3. I am walking in the power you have given me to get wealth (Deuteronomy 8:18), and *I am increasing in wisdom, status, and in favor with God and with men* according to Luke 2:52. I am the apple of God's eye (Psalm 17:8), and I am reigning as a king and walking in divine favor. I commit myself to read, meditate, and ponder on the Word of God until my thoughts become the thoughts of God. I have the peace Jesus has given me concerning my business, ministry, or anything I put my hands to do. I rejoice in the fact that I am *the man who walks, not in the counsel of the ungodly, nor sits in the seat of the scornful, but I delight myself in the Lord* according to Psalm 1:1. This is my season of abundant and great success; supernatural doors are flying open. I come against any satanic and demonic activity that is set up to interfere with my success *(Pray in the Holy Spirit and clap your hands)*. Satan, I speak to you, and I say, "*enough is enough*" Every witch, warlock, third eye, black magic, sorcery, voodoo, plague, spirit of limbo, and spirit of emptier that has been sent out to hinder my success, I call forth the consuming fire of God to destroy you *(Pray in the Holy Spirit and clap your hands)*. I release the angelic hosts of God to intervene on my behalf, open doors, and bring me an idea that will change my life forever. I believe today, I will never be broke another day in my life *(Pray in the Holy Spirit and clap your hands)*. Amen!

BONUS CONFESSIONS

Standing in the Gap for our Leaders (Government)

The Word of God tells us *that all authorities come from God, and those who are in power over us have been placed there by God. So, anyone who rebels against the authority is rebelling against God, and those who rebel will be punished by Him* according to Romans 13:1-3 (NLT). God has commanded believers to pray for the government leaders, and anyone who has the authority over us. In Genesis 1:26, the Bible says, "God has given us dominion and authority to rule this earth." One way believers rule is through their prayers. Every believer should intercede in prayer for the government of their nation, regardless of what political party is in power. The Bible says, "He controls the course of the world events; he removes kings and sets up other kings" (Daniel 2:21 NLT). So, God is not surprised with who is voted into office because He is the one who puts one in and takes one out.

Our responsibility here on earth is to pray God's will to come to earth as it is in heaven. Here is a fundamental truth; every born-again believer should keep in mind that we belong first to the kingdom of God. We do not belong to this world or a political party of this world's system. If the believer's mind is not renewed, then the believer will be conformed to this world and will miss what God is doing in our government.

The Word of God says, "For unto us a child is born, unto us a son is given, and the government shall be upon His shoulder, and His name shall be called Wonderful, Counselor, The Mighty God, The Everlasting Father, The Prince of Peace," Isaiah 9:6 (KJV). The government of any country is on the shoulders of the believers because *as Jesus is, so are we in this world* (I John 4:17). If the believer doesn't rule his or her world, then Satan will rule instead. Prayer for our government is our responsibility, regardless of who is in power.

Confession for our Leaders (Government)

Father, in the name of Jesus, I choose to stand in the authority Jesus has given me, and I intercede on behalf of those who are in authority in the country of (fill in the name of the country here). I pray for all leaders in the government who are in high and low positions that your peace rules in everything they put their hands to do concerning our government. I lift up our President, Vice President, all members of the Cabinet, Justices of the Supreme Court, and every lawmaker before you now and their families. Father, your Word says, *The king's heart is in your hands, and you will turn it wherever you please* (Proverbs 21:1). I ask that you will turn their hearts to please you today. According to Mark 3:25, *a house divided among itself cannot stand*. I take authority over every spirit of division; I bind it now *(Pray in the Holy Spirit and clap your hands)*. I loose unity among the lawmakers in Jesus' name. I declare and decree they have a heart for your people and not their own selfish ambition. I release godly wisdom and understanding over the President, Vice President, and every member of their Cabinet. I decree they are people of integrity, character, honor, and they serve the Lord and fear Him.

Father, I ask you that those in authority who do not have a heart for your people will be exposed and cut off from our government. I decree that our government makes righteous laws, and our nation is prosperous in all it puts its hands to do.

Jehovah, my covenant-keeping God, your Word commands us to *pray for the peace of Jerusalem; we pray that there will be peace within her walls, and I declare prosperity is in her palaces* (Psalm 122:6-7). I declare our President will seek to be friends and come to the aid of Jerusalem, and when *the enemy comes into the walls of Jerusalem like a flood*, I decree and declare *the spirit of the Lord will lift up a standard against him* according to Isaiah 59:19 *(Pray in the Holy Spirit and clap your hands).*

I ask that this nation will be at peace, and that this is a nation that is marked with goodness and dignity. Father, your Word says, *If your people who are called by your name should humble themselves and pray and seek you, and turn from their wicked ways, you will hear from heaven, and you will forgive their sins and heal their land* according to II Chronicles 7:14. Therefore, I repent for the sins of this nation. Forgive us, Master, for we have sinned against you. *Arise, O Lord and have mercy and compassion on* (fill in the name of the country here), *for it is time to show favor to her* (Psalm 102:13). I decree this country's appointed time has come, and our government is free from corruption. I call forth righteousness because your Word says, *When the righteous are in charge, the earth rejoice* (Proverbs 29:2). I thank you that our leaders are men and women after your own heart.

Our government is stable, and because we have a stable government, our nation is healthy and is the most powerful nation on the earth because this nation loves you and will follow your Word in Jesus' name. Amen!

Breaking Free From the Spirit of Homosexuality

We are certainly in the last days, and it seems as though sin and iniquity have crept into our societies much more than usual. But, the Bible tells us, *Where sin abounds, grace much more abounds* according to Romans 5:20. If we go back to the Bible days, we see that Sodom and Gomorrah and the city of Benjamin were destroyed because of the sin of homosexuality. In fact, Leviticus 18:22 (NLT) declares, "Do not practice homosexuality, having sex with another man as with a woman. It is a detestable sin." When God created the Garden of Eden, He wanted a family, so He created Adam, and then from Adam, God created Eve. God told Adam and Eve to be *fruitful and multiply and replenish the earth* (Genesis 1:28). The word multiply in the Hebrew dictionary is *rawbaw*—it means to become numerous or become much. Adam and Eve were to become numerous. Therefore, this was the original intent for man to multiply and become fruitful.

God's order for marriage is very clear, and anything else outside of this is considered a disorder. The Word of God says, *The wages of sin is death, but the free gift of God is eternal life* (Romans 6:23). If a person dies while living a homosexual lifestyle, or any other sin without repentance, the payment of their sin is eternal death. This spiritual death symbolizes eternity away from the presence of God. But, God's will *is that none will perish, but all should come to repentance* (II Peter 3:9). As believers, we should love and stand in the gap for our friends, family, or anyone we come in contact with until deliverance takes place. Remember, it is with *lovingkindness they are drawn,* not with a judgmental spirit (Jeremiah 31:3).

If you are reading this book, and you are living a lifestyle of homosexuality, I want you to know God loves you so much. He sent His Son over two thousand years ago, and you have already been set free! But, you must receive what he has done by faith. Cry out to Jesus right where you are. He will come right there in your midst! The Word of God says, *If you call on the name of the Lord, you will be saved* (Romans 10:13).

Confession for Breaking Homosexuality

I put on right now the whole armor of God. I put on the belt of truth, the breastplate of righteousness, the preparation of the gospel of peace, the shield of faith, the helmet of salvation, and I pick up the sword of the spirit (Ephesians 6:13-17), and wage war against the enemy for the life of (fill in the name(s) here), in Jesus' name. I declare *no weapon that has been formed against* (fill in the name(s) here) *will prosper* according to Isaiah 54:17.

Father, I believe by faith when I call on you, you will hear me and will answer me. So I am calling on you on behalf of (fill the name(s) here). I come against the spirit of homosexuality that has attached itself to his/ her life. I bind, (forbid, declare you to be improper and unlawful) trespassing in the body of (fill in the name (s) here). I loose you and command you to flee now in the name of Jesus according to Matthew 18:18 (AMP) *(Pray in the Holy Spirit and clap your hands)*. You, spirit of perversion, lust, and impurity, the Lord rebuke you *(Pray in the Holy Spirit or clap your hands).* I speak to every satanic and demonic plan against the life of (fill in the name(s) here). I break your hold *(Pray in the Holy Spirit or clap your hands)*. I stand in my authority Jesus has given me, *and I command the veil to be lifted from the mind of* (fill in the name(s) here). I command his/her ears and eyes to be opened to the truth of God's Word (II Corinthians 4:4).

Satan, *I spoil your house* according to Matthew 12:29, and I enter in and bind your hands in the life of (fill in the name(s) here). I command the chains that are holding him/her to fall in the name of Jesus. I speak to the spirit of homosexuality, and I command you to leave the life of (fill in the name(s) here) *(Speak in the Holy Spirit and clap your hands).*

Father, I thank you because (fill in the name(s) here) ways are pleasing to you, and he/she is holy as you are holy. I believe (fill in the name(s) here) is saved, his/her mind is renewed, and he/she is filled with the Holy Spirit.

I pray that you will give (fill in the name(s) here) spiritual insight, so he/she might grow in the *knowledge of you, and that you will flood* his/her *heart with the light of your glory, so that* he/she *will understand and have the confidence and hope of who you called* him/her *to be in Christ Jesus, our Lord,* according to Ephesians 1:17-18, in Jesus' name. Amen!

Overcoming the Spirit of Depression

Depression is a demonic spirit, and it is serious business. When the spirit of depression oppresses an individual, it opens the door to the spirit of suicide. Both of these spirits are demonic, and their purpose is to lead the individual to eventually take their own life. An individual who is oppressed by the spirits of depression and suicide needs deliverance.

In the past few weeks right here in America, two prominent people took their own lives. It's very alarming because most people who deal with this spirit of depression show no signs of being depressed on the outside. In fact, the people who love them can't tell they are depressed. Many of them are on anti-depressive medicine, which works to suppress their moods, emotions, and it helps the individual sleep better, increase their appetite and concentration.

Maybe you are reading this, and you are dealing with this spirit called depression. I want you to know Jesus has already defeated the spirit of depression. As a believer, you must understand Jesus has already paid the price, and because he did, you are already free. The Word of God says, according to I Peter 2:24 (NLT), "He personally carried our sins in his body on the cross so that we can be dead to sin and live for what is right. By his wounds you are healed." So, healing belongs to you, and whatever your need or whatever problems you may be facing today, you can call on the Lord, and the Bible says, *He will answer you* (Psalm 91:15).

One of the fruits of the spirit is joy; I believe joy is the fruit of an overcomer. The Bible tells us that, *The joy of the LORD is your strength* (Nehemiah 8:10). Laughter is an excellent medicine for your soul. It's time you sat down and began to think about the good times in your life and just laugh. In fact, you should begin to laugh at the plans of the enemy because you know his plans will not work.

Hence, right there in the middle of what you are going through, call on the Lord and ask Him to help you! The Bible says, "Ask and it shall be given to you; seek and you shall find; knock and the door shall be opened to you. For everyone that asks receives; the one who seeks finds; and to the one who knocks, the door will be opened," (Matthew 7:7-8 NIV).

The Holy Spirit will tell you what to do and divinely connect you to the right people. Don't walk through what you are going through alone. The Bible says you can *look to the hills—where your help comes from. Your help comes from the Lord"* (Psalm 121:1-2). *The Lord will not let you stumble* (Psalm 37:24), and He *will not put you to shame* (Psalm 25:3). I want you to know Jesus loves you, and He is with you because His Word says, *He will never leave you nor forsake you* (Hebrews 13:5). Open your mouth right there where you are and call out the name, Jesus! He will answer you!

Confession for Overcoming Depression

Jesus, I need you. You said I can come to you when I am weary and carrying a heavy burden, and you said you will give me rest (Matthew 11:28). Father, I admit today I need rest. I can't carry this load, so I lay my (speak the load to the Lord here) down at your feet. I speak to the spirit of depression that has been oppressing me, and I denounce you *(Pray in the Holy Spirit or clap your hands)*. My body is the temple of the Holy Spirit, and I present my body holy and acceptable to you, Lord, *which is my reasonable service* (Romans 12:1). I speak to my soul (mind, will, and emotions), and I command you to find rest in God alone. My hope comes from you.

IF YOU CHANGE YOUR WORDS, YOU'LL CHANGE YOUR LIFE!

Surely, Jesus has taken depression away from me, *and by His stripes, I am healed* (Isaiah 53:5) *(Pray in the Holy Spirit or clap your hands)*. Father, your Word says that *you are a shelter for the oppressed, a refuge in time of trouble, and those who know your name trust in you, for you Lord, do not abandon those who search for you* according to Psalm 9:9-10. I search for you, and I trust that you, Lord, will shelter me in times of trouble. The greater one lives on the inside of me, so I am already victorious.

Thank you, Jehovah Rapha. You are the God that healed me, and all my hope is built on you alone. Father, your Word says that *you are close to the brokenhearted and save those who are crushed in spirit* according to Psalm 34:18. I believe right now my broken heart is healed, and I have *overcome by the blood of the lamb and the word of my testimony* (Revelation 12:11). I testify that I am healed because over two thousand years ago Jesus paid the price for me. So, I am free. I thank you, Father, in advance, that the spirit of depression's power has been broken over me *(Pray in the Holy Spirit or clap your hands)*. Thank you for *renewing my strength and causing me to mount up with wings like an eagle* according to Isaiah 40:31. Amen!

Defeating Loneliness

I can't tell you how many young believers I have met in the last year who battle day to day with loneliness. Loneliness is real. Not only do single people deal with it, but some people who are married, do, too. When a person deals with loneliness, they tend to get involved in relationships and other things that drive them away from the will of God. They get involved because they are trying to fill a void in their lives, which in the end only becomes a temporary fix for the real thing they desire. Many young people who are lonely turn to sex outside of marriage, drugs, masturbation, pornography, and attend sinful parties to fill the void in their lives. The enemy offers a temporary fix, which can lead the person's life to destruction.

I believe the missing link for anyone who deals with loneliness is a lack of identity. I am not saying the isolation they feel is not real, and there is no need to desire a spouse. But what I am saying is the void is an indicator the individual doesn't know what his or her true purpose is. So these ungodly substitutions become a hindrance. Also, I came to discover what is missing in their lives is an intimate relationship with God!

Once, we pursue our relationship with the Father through intimacy, we will discover our true identity and live a life of purpose. After this discovery is made, this will lead the individual to find fulfillment. Have you ever seen a person who has a purpose-driven life? They have no time to waste; they are always busy, working, and pursuing what they discovered about themselves. When they found what they love, they do it with all their heart. This discovery opens the door to a life of purpose, and when they are busy with purpose, the right one will come when they least expect it!

Confession for Defeating Loneliness

Father, I confess now that I am an overcomer, *and no temptation is subject to me that you have not already made a way out for me to escape it* according to I Corinthians 10:13. I have walked contrary to your Word, and I confess that I have fallen into the sin of (fill in here). I repent. I change my mind, and I turn away now from it. Father, I have to admit I have been lonely. But, I know your Word declares, *When my father and mother abandon me, you will take me* (Psalm 27:10). Take my hands and lead me into your secret place, so I can discover who I am in you. Place within me a desire to seek your face daily, so I can be where you are. Fill the void and deep longings of my heart and help me to love you more. Father, call me deeper *in my dry and barren life, where there is no water; let me see your power and your glory* according to Psalm 63:1-2. "Turn to me and be gracious to me, for I am lonely and afflicted," (Psalm 25:16 NLT). "Restore to me the joy of your salvation and give me a willing spirit to obey you," (Psalm 51:12 NLT).

Jehovah God, *lead me not into temptation but deliver me from all evil* (Matthew 6:13), so the world may know that you are my God. I know you are with me when no one is around to hold my hand and brighten up my way. Open my eyes and let me see the path you have set before me. Help me, Father, to rest in your Word for my life, *for you know the thoughts you think towards me; it is a plan of good and not of evil, to take me to my expected end* according to Jeremiah 29:11. I give you glory because *you have already given me my heart's desire because I am delighting myself in you* (Psalm 37:4), in Jesus' name *(Pray in the Holy Spirit or clap your hands)*. Amen!

Emergency Numbers

Repentance	General Confession	Spiritual Warfare	Uncertainties
I John 1:9	Ephesians 6:12	Genesis 1:26	Isaiah 41:10
Acts 3:19	Romans 12:1	Isaiah 14:13-14	Psalm 40:1-3
II Chronicles 7:14	Daniel 10:13	Ephesians 6:12-17	Jeremiah 29:11
Proverbs 28:13	Isaiah 61:1	II Corinthians 10:5	John 16:33
James 4:8-10	Luke 2:52	Matthew 18:18	Romans 8:31
Psalm 51:1-4	Deuteronomy 28:12	Isaiah 54:17	II Timothy 1:7
Hebrew 11:6	Ephesians 6:10-18	Ezekiel 28:13	Hebrew 13:5
Jonah 1,2	I Corinthians 4:10	Revelation 12:7-9	Philippians 4:8
James 5:16	Galatians 3:29	Hebrews 12:29	Proverbs 18:21; 11:21
Psalm 139:23-24			
Staying Consistent During testing	**When Enemies Rise up Against me**	**Temptation**	**Purpose and Destiny**
Genesis 22	Hebrew 1:13	James 1:12	Jeremiah 1:5
I Peter 4:12-13	Deuteronomy 28:7	James 4:7	Psalm 139:13
I Corinthians 10:13	Exodus 23:22	Luke 11:4	Jeremiah 29:11
II Corinthians 5:7	Leviticus 26:6	I Corinthians 10:13	Isaiah 14:24
I Corinthians 6:18	Proverbs 16:7	Matthew 26:41NLT	Habakkuk 2:3
Psalm 118:24	Psalm 23:5	Matthew 6:13	Romans 8:28
Romans 8:37	Isaiah 59:19	Romans 12:12	Proverbs 19:21
I John 5:4-5		Philippians 4:13	Ephesians 3:20
James 1:2-5,12			Exodus 9:16
			Isaiah 42:6
Desiring to Have Children	**Marriage Made in Heaven**	**Desiring to be Married**	**Praying for Children**
Psalm 127:3-5	Proverbs 3:5-6; 31	Proverbs 18:21	Proverbs 22:6
Psalm 113:9	Ecclesiastes 4:12	Psalm 37:4	Proverbs 13:24; 13:1
Genesis 25: 21	Mark 10:9	Genesis 2:18	Ephesians 6:4
Psalm 84: 11	I Peter 4:8	Hebrew 10:38	Joel 2:28
Exodus 23:26 AMP.	Ephesians 4:2-3	Mark 11:24	Isaiah 54:13; 32:17
Acts 10:34	Ephesians 4:32;5:25	Hebrew 11:1	Jeremiah 31:16
Psalm 138:8	I John 4:7-8	II Peter 1:3	Psalm 138:8
I John 5:14-15	Romans 8:32 12;10	Isaiah 54:5	Psalm 141:3-4
Deuteronomy 28:11	Colossians 3:14	Ecclesiastes 4:9-11	I Peter 2:9
	Proverbs 18:22		

IF YOU CHANGE YOUR WORDS, YOU'LL CHANGE YOUR LIFE!

Strongholds	Debt Freedom	Tithing	Kingdom Prosperity
Proverbs 23:7	Romans 13:8	Malachi 3:8-10	Psalm 112
II Corinthians 10:3-4	Proverbs 22:7	Haggai 2:5-9	Matthew 6:33
Matthew 11:12	Mark 11:23	I Corinthians 3:6	Psalm 35:27; 68:19
Revelation 12:11	Colossians 2:14	Leviticus 27:30	Joshua 1:8
Psalm 34:19	Galatians 6:9	Deuteronomy 26:1-2	Deuteronomy 8:6-18
Matthew 18:18	Galatians 5:1	Matthew 22:21	Isaiah 55:11
	Matthew 6:33	Psalm 2:6-8	II Corinthians 9
	Proverbs 11:28-29	Hebrews 7: 4-8	Mark 4:24-25
	Psalm 37:21	Proverbs 3:9-10	Genesis 1:22
		Deuteronomy 30:9	Proverbs 10:22
		Genesis 12:1-3	
Sowing and Reaping	**Living In God's Righteousness**	**Spiritual Revelation**	**Walking in God's Favor**
Genesis 8:22	Romans 5:17	Proverbs 4:20-27	Luke 2:52
Ecclesiastes 11:1-4	Acts 17:28	Psalm 119:18	Genesis 6:8
Proverbs 10:5	Philippians 3:9	Ephesians 1:17-23	I Samuel 2:26
Proverbs 6:6-8	I Corinthians 1:30	Proverbs 4:5-10	Proverbs 12:2
Galatians 6:7	II Corinthians 5:21	Colossians 1:9-10	Proverbs 18:22
Mark 4:26-29	1 Peter 3:12	Ephesians 3:14-20	Numbers 6:25
Galatians 6:9	Isaiah 32:17	Proverbs 1	Psalm 67:1; 89:17
Psalm 1	James 5:16	Psalm 119:97-99	Psalm 30:5; 90:17
Jeremiah 17:7-8	Proverbs 11:21; 12:3		Psalm 84:11
Jeremiah 5:24	Romans 10:1-10		
	Isaiah 54:14-17		
	Romans 3:21-22		
Finding a Job	**Business**	**Desiring a House**	**Strength**
II Thessalonians 3:10	Deuteronomy 8:18	Joshua 24:13	Isaiah 40: 29; 31
John 14:14; 15:7	Deuteronomy 28:2	Exodus 6:8	Ephesians 6:10
Philippians 4:19 4:13	I Peter 4:10	Isaiah 32:18	Philippians 4:13
Psalm 90:16,17	Psalm 112:5	Philippians 4:19	II Corinthians 12:9
Luke 11:9	Joshua 1:9	Psalm 107:7	Psalm 46:1; 22:19
John 14:13	Proverbs 4:20-27	Proverbs 15:6	Psalm 28:7-8; 118:14
Isaiah 40:31; 43: 19	Luke 2:52	Proverbs 24:3-4	Isaiah 12:2
Ecclesiastes 9:10	Psalm 90:17	Matthew 19:29-30	Habakkuk 3:19
Proverbs 21:1	I Corinthians 4:5	Deuteronomy 6:11	Psalm 73:26
Psalm 37:25; 23:1	Proverbs 3:3-5		

EMERGENCY NUMBERS

The Peace of God	Comfort During Loss	Praying for Government	Praying for Leaders
Colossians 3:15	Isaiah 53:4	Psalm 2:8; 33:12	Ephesians 1:17-23
James 3:18	Psalm 119:28	Proverbs 21:1; 29:2	Luke 2:52
Philippians 4:7	Revelation 21:4	I Timothy 2:1-2	John 3:30
Psalm 29:11	Psalm 34:18	II Thessalonians 3:1-2	Proverbs 11:4
Romans 12:18; 14:19	John 14:1	II Chronicles 7:14	Daniel 9:17
Psalm 34:14; 37:7	Matthew 5:4	Proverbs 22:28; 21:1	Proverbs 29:14; 4:23
Psalm 85:5; 119:165	Psalm 30:5	Daniel 2:21	Jeremiah 17:7-8
Isaiah 26:3	Hebrews 12:1	Mark 3:25	Galatians 6:9
John 16:33; 14:27		I Peter 2:17	Roman 13:1-4
II Thessalonians 3:16		Isaiah 9:6	Proverbs 21:1
		Psalm 2:10-11	

Living in Good Health	Breaking Addiction	Breaking the Spirit of Depression	Shame
III John 1:2	John 8:32	Psalm 143:3-10	Isaiah 50:7
I Timothy 4:7-9	Romans 6:16	Ecclesiastes 7:17	Isaiah 61:7
Proverbs 3:7-8;16:24	Romans 13:14	Jeremiah 29:11	Luke 9:26
Psalm 63:5	I Corinthians 6:12	Deuteronomy 30:19	Mark 8:38
I Corinthians 6:19-20	I Corinthians 10:13	John 10:10	Romans 8:31
I Corinthians 10:31	James 4:7	II Corinthians 10:4-5	Proverbs 13:1
Proverbs 17:22	II Corinthians 5:17	Isaiah 26:3	Isaiah 45:16
Jeremiah 33:6	Philippians 4:13	I John 4:16	Job 8:22
Proverbs 4:20-27	I John 2:16		Psalm 25:2
Proverbs 3:24			

Defending Healing	Confession for a Backslider	Letting Go of the Past	Breaking from the Spirit of Fear
Matthew 8:17	Jeremiah 3:22	Philippians 3:7-9	I John 4:18
Exodus 15:26	Jeremiah 3:12	John 1:12	II Timothy 1:7
Exodus 23:25-26	Proverbs 14:14	Psalm 23:5	Psalm 23:4
Hebrews 10:17	Proverbs 24:16	Philippians 3:13	Philippians 4:8
Isaiah 53:4-5	Hosea 14:1	Galatians 2:20	Psalm 46:1
Psalm 103:3	Jeremiah 24:7	Proverbs 3:5:6	John 4:4
Psalm 107:20	Jeremiah 3:14	Philippians 3:10-11	Matthew 18:18
Psalm 34:19		Romans 6:4	John 8:36
Jeremiah 30:17		Philippians 3:12-14	
Malachi 4:2			
I Peter 2:24			
Nahum 1:9			

IF YOU CHANGE YOUR WORDS, YOU'LL CHANGE YOUR LIFE!

Unsaved Love Ones	Walking in Divine Protection	Breaking the Spirit of Homosexuality	Defeating Unbelief, Doubt, and Frustration
II Peter 3:9	Psalm 91	Ephesians 6:11-17	Hebrew 10:38
Matthew 18:18	Psalm 46:1; 20:1	Isaiah 54:17	I John 4:4
Matthew 9:37-38	Psalm 23; 34:19	Isaiah 65:24	II Corinthians 4:13
II Timothy 2:26	Psalm 118:17	Matthew 18:18	Mark 11:23
Jeremiah 1:12	II Thessalonians 3:3	II Corinthians 4:4	II Corinthians 5:7
Isaiah 55:11	Isaiah 41:10	Matthew 12:29	Isaiah 54:17
Philippians 1:6	Ephesians 6:11	Proverbs 16:7	Ephesians 6:11-17
	Deuteronomy 31:6	John 8:36	
		Ephesians 1:17-19	

Contact Information

P.O. Box 22
Clarksburg, Maryland 20871
Email: Maxineryan48@gmail.com

Other book by Maxine Ryan

Do you want to grow in your faith, while
being transformed in the Word of God?
This book is for you. Many who read it,
say they can't put it down!
Purchase today on Amazon.

www.ingramcontent.com/pod-product-compliance
Lightning Source LLC
Chambersburg PA
CBHW030323080526
44584CB00012B/688